Pro Lege Rege et Grege

Perth & Kinross

A Pocket Miscellany

A Companion for Visitors and Residents

Trish Colton

*with illustrations by Rob Hands
and photographs by Roben Antoniewicz*

TIPPERMUIR
· BOOKS LIMITED ·

Editorial and Project Director: Paul S. Philippou.
Editorial Assistance:
Jean Hands, Alan Laing, Matthew Mackie, and Steve Zajda.

Illustrations: Rob Hands.
Additional Illustrations: DougEye ('Wolf' and 'White-tailed Eagle').
Photographs: Roben Antoniewicz.
Additional Photographs:
Rosser1954 (*Loch Tay, reconstructed crannog at the
Scottish Crannog Centre*), Ewen Rennie (*Orwell Standing Stones* and
Clach Ossian, Sma Glen), Martin Loader (*Witches Stone, nr Meikle Obney*)–
licensed under the Creative Commons Attribution-ShareAlike 4.0
International License.

Cover Design: Matthew Mackie.
Cover illustration: *The City of Perth*, from the "69 Cities of the UK" project
by Carl Lavia and Lorna Le Bredonchel.
Text Design, Layout and artwork by Bernard Chandler [graffik]

ISBN: 978-1-9164778-0-3 (paperback).
A CIP catalogue record for this book is available from the British Library.

Text set in Utopia Std 10.2pt on 13pt.
Printed and bound by CPI Group (UK) Ltd, Croydon, CRO 4YY.

ACKNOWLEDGEMENTS

THERE ARE LOTS OF PEOPLE for me to thank, not least all those whose earlier research has enabled me to write this book at all. As you will see from the Bibliography, they are many.

I should also especially like to thank Susan Beech of Fife Walking, Neil Laird of Scottish Golf History and Jon Plunkett of the Corbenic Poetry Path, all of whom kindly allowed me to use extracts from their websites.

Everyone from Tippermuir Books has been particularly kind and supportive, which has been greatly appreciated. My special thanks to Roben Antoniewicz, Dougie Hamilton and Rob Hands for their wonderful illustrations and photographs. Jean Hands, Alan Laing and Steve Zajda for their careful proofing of the book; Carl Lavia, Lorna Le Bredonchel, and Matthew Mackie for the lovely book cover. And not forgetting Paul Philippou, whose editing skills and enormous patience has been fantastic.

And last, but not least, a big thank you to Carole, Barrie and Bob for all their encouragement.

CONTENTS

PERTH & KINROSS

TODAY, Scotland is divided into council areas, but it wasn't always that way. Malcolm III, who reigned from 1058 to 1093, was fed up with the system the Normans had introduced, so he changed it and brought in sheriffdoms instead. Subsequent rulers liked the idea and David I, who reigned 1124-53, completed the process by changing the remaining 'thanedoms' into 'sheriffdoms'. This heralded the beginning of our 'shires' and by the time Edward I issued his Ordinance for the Government of Scotland in 1305, there were 23 to be listed in it, including both Perth & Kinross.

Things changed again with the Acts of Union, passed by the English and Scottish Parliaments in 1706 and 1707 respectively. By then, some of the offices of sheriff had become hereditary. When George II ascended the throne in 1727, this applied to 22 of them, including Kinross. In Perth the appointment was held only for life.

Following further administrative changes over the years, the Local Government (Scotland) Act 1929 finally saw Perth & Kinross joined together for the first time as a joint county council. Despite this, in May 1973, counties were replaced by regions and districts, with a further reorganisation in 1994 replacing them with the council areas we have now, including Perth & Kinross Council.

Note: Even though it would be more accurate to use the terms 'County of Perth' and 'County of Kinross', I have used the more familiar 'Perthshire' and 'Kinross-shire' when naming a specific county.

LIST OF ILLUSTRATIONS

[1] ©Rosser1954
[2] ©Ewen Rennie
[3] ©Martin Loader
[4] ©Ewen Rennie

'Life is all a variorum'

Late fifth to the mid-fourth millennium BC:
Cleaven Dyke built. This is a Neolithic bank stretching just under a mile in length, northeast of the village of Meikleour.

500 BC Crannogs begin appearing on lochs throughout Perth & Kinross.

AD 80-200 Ardoch Roman Camp built and occupied.

AD 83 or 84 Battle of Mons Graupius (if it really took place).

AD 800 The Dunfallandy Stone erected but carved sometime in the 700s. This elaborately carved Pictish cross slab can be seen today, protected from the elements, about a mile south of the centre of Pitlochry, near a farm.

1126-8 St John's Kirk mentioned in a document by David I.

c.1150 Perth's Lade constructed to act as part of the city's defences. It meant that Perth was surrounded by substantial water courses, with the River Tay on one side and the Lade surrounding the rest of the city.

1260 Work starts on building Dunkeld Cathedral.

1286 Alexander III's heart buried in St John's Kirk following his accidental death in Fife.

c.1300 Loch Leven Castle, Kinross, built.

1303 William Wallace reputed to have captured Loch Leven Castle, killing all 30 English soldiers garrisoned there, plus the five women who were also in the castle at the time.

1306 Battle of Methven. Robert the Bruce's fledgling army defeated by Edward I's army under Aymer de Valence in the First War of Scottish Independence.

1313 Having recaptured Perth, Robert the Bruce stays at Loch Leven Castle.

1332 Battle of Dupplin Moor. Second War of Scottish Independence fought between supporters of the infant David II, four-year-old son of Robert the Bruce, and rebels supporting the Balliol claim.

1392 Battle of the Clans (North Inch, Perth).

15th century Huntingtower Castle built (then known as the House of Ruthven).

1437 James I murdered in Perth.

c.1450-1502 Golf began to be played on what is one of the oldest golf courses in the world – the North Inch Golf Course.

1452 Castle Huntly (now HMP Castle Huntly, an open prison) built.

c.1475 Original Fair Maid's House built.

1513 Leader of the Protestant Reformation, John Knox, born.

1534 James, Earl of Bothwell, born.

1540 Kinross made a Burgh of Barony by James V (as distinct from a Royal Burgh). This gave the landowner the right to hold weekly markets, but not to participate in foreign trade, which a Royal Burgh could do.

1542 Mary, Queen of Scots, born.

1545 Henry Stuart (Lord Darnley) born.

1563 John Knox visits Mary, Queen of Scots, at Loch Leven Castle.

1567 Mary, Queen of Scots, imprisoned at Loch Leven Castle.

1567 Mary, Queen of Scots, 'persuaded' to abdicate during her imprisonment at Loch Leven Castle.

1573 Pacification of Perth.

1657 According to legend, Maggie Wall burned as a witch.

1680 Innerpeffray Library established.

1680 Kinross begins to develop cutlery and ironmongery manufacturing industries.

1689 Battle of Killiecrankie. The first major engagement in the Jacobite Risings. The notorious Rob Roy MacGregor is associated with the battle.

1689 Battle of Dunkeld fought between Jacobites and Covenanters.

1753   Dalguise House built, where Beatrix Potter went on holiday as a child and teenager.

1758   Ossian's Hall, at the Hermitage, near Dunkeld, constructed.

1805   Scone Palace built.

1809   Thomas Telford builds a new bridge at Dunkeld.

1838   A. K. Bell Library (building) constructed.

c.1840   The present harbour in Perth built. Earlier harbours were much further upstream, as far as the High Street. As the river became less navigable, particularly with ships getting larger and the River Tay silting up, the harbour moved further and further downstream until the present harbour was built at Friarton, which was designed by the grandfather and uncle of novelist and poet Robert Louis Stevenson.

1847   The railway arrives in Perthshire.

1914   Suffragettes attempt to disrupt George V's visit to Perth.

1929   Perthshire and Kinross-shire share a joint county council.

1996   Perth & Kinross Council formed with the division of Tayside region into three new unitary council areas: Perth & Kinross, Angus and Dundee City.

2001   The population of Perth reaches 43,450, five times larger than in 1770.

2004   The population of Kinross grows to 4,580, almost tenfold that of 1710, when it was 476.

2012   Perth regains its city status.

'O thou! Whatever title suit thee'

1 King James VI Golf Club is Scotland's only self-contained golf course situated on a river island – Moncreiffe Island in the River Tay at Perth.

2 The first inter-club golf match is believed to have been played between King James VI Golf Club and Elie & Earlsferry Golf Club in 1860.

3 Legend has it that Mary, Queen of Scots, played golf.

4 Apparently, King Arthur and his wife Guinevere came from Perthshire, not the West of England. One member of the collection of Pictish stones in the Meigle Sculptured Stone Museum is known as 'Vanora's Stone'. Vanora is a variant of Guinevere and not only does this stone have her name on it, together with some others it is said to have formed a memorial to the lady.

5 There are a number of stories linking King Arthur with this part of Scotland. For example, Guinevere is said to have been imprisoned in the prehistoric fort on top of Barry Hill, near both Dunkeld and Birnam, for falling in love with a Pictish prince.

6 Loch Leven used to be a lot bigger than it is today. Following the construction of a drainage canal in the nineteenth century, the water level fell by about 4 feet 6 inches – or in some accounts it dropped by 9 feet. Whichever it was, Castle Island, where Mary, Queen of Scots, was imprisoned, was considerably smaller during her time there because the water level was higher.

7 The reduction in Loch Leven's water level meant that salmon and sea trout disappeared from the loch. Pike almost disappeared too, but that was due to a deliberate effort to get rid of them at the beginning of the twentieth century to protect the freshwater trout. (In 1903, 14,000 pike were removed by netting).

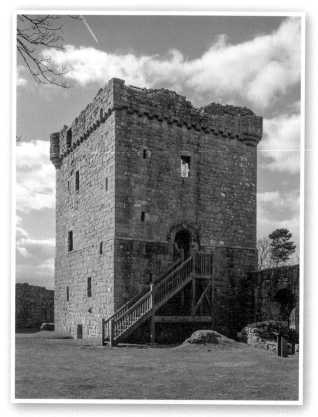

8 A medieval silver crucifix was found when Loch Leven's water level was reduced, so too was an ancient log canoe.

9 Perth was the first town in Scotland to hold a regular farmers' market.

10 The water at St Conval's Well, beside the road near Huntingtower Castle, is said to have healing powers. But it won't work unless you stay absolutely silent on your journey to and from the well to collect it.

11 In the nineteenth century, there were more than 2,000 lochs and ponds in Scotland where curling was played.

12 At the time of writing, there are 63 curling clubs in Perthshire.

13 Curling was first played in Scotland 500 years ago.

14 The oldest extant curling stone (with the date 1511 engraved on it) was found at the bottom of Lake Menteith.

15 Through the course of this book, the Earl of Atholl is sometimes referred to as the Duke of Atholl. Which title is used depends on which point in history is being written about. The title changed from Earl to Duke when the latter title was bestowed on the Second Marquis of Atholl by Queen Anne in 1703.

16 In 1567, Mary, Queen of Scots, was forced to abdicate in favour of her infant son James VI after she was imprisoned in Loch Leven Castle. Almost a year later, she escaped. Following defeat at the Battle of Langside, Mary fled to England where she was eventually executed. As the Scottish king was only a baby when she abdicated, the kingdom had to be ruled by a regent, but over the course of the next seven years there was a run of four of them. There was also intermittent civil war between the king's forces and those of Queen Mary. In 1573, the English ambassador brokered a meeting between the two sides which was held in Perth – the 'Pacification of Perth'. Agreement was reached to recognise James Douglas, 4th Earl of Morton, as regent and to end any further allegiance to Mary. The rebels were allowed to keep their lands. All of this was important because there was now no chance of Mary regaining her throne, should she ever return. It also created a period of stability.

17 Ireland's 1840s potato famine is well known. What is lesser known however, is that potato blight also hit Scotland, including Highland Perthshire, in 1846. According to Scotland's most famous historian, Tom Devine, the famine lasted for a much longer period here than it did in Ireland. It endured for a further eight or nine years. People were saved from starvation by massive charitable intervention.

18 The geographical centre of Scotland is reckoned to lie in Highland Perthshire, on the shoulder of Schiehallion, a Munro located about 10 miles to the west-north-west of Aberfeldy.

19 Towards the end of the Ice Age, the sea reached almost as far as Crieff, thanks to a channel which carried it from Perth, then on the coast.

20 The M90 is the northernmost motorway in the UK, which makes Craigend Interchange, south of Perth, the northernmost complex interchange.

21 The Kinross bypass, which opened in 1972, was the first motorway to be built using a concrete surface.

22 Kinross Services are the most northerly motorway services in Britain, being located just off Junction 6 of the M90.

23 Castle Huntly, at Longforgan in the Carse of Gowrie, is Scotland's only open prison. It accommodates 285 low supervision adult male offenders from any Scottish local authority area.

24 Perth Prison is the oldest occupied prison in Scotland. It was also the first prison in Britain to hold a non-public execution in 1870 when George Chalmers, a vagrant from Braco, was hanged there. Public executions had been abolished in 1868.

25 Scotland's largest waterwheel is on view at Keathbank Mill, Blairgowrie. It is just over 14 feet wide and just over 18 feet in diameter.

26 The unusual crown tower of St Leonards-in-the-Fields church, by Perth's South Inch, is probably the first such tower to be built in post-Reformation Scotland.

27 The Roman name for the River Tay was the 'Tava'.

28 It is probable that a Celtic tribe called the 'Venicones' lived in southern Perthshire and Kinross-shire (and may well have extended into Fife).

29 There are 73 towns and villages in Perth & Kinross.

30 One of the late Queen Mother's tiaras is known as the Strathmore Rose Tiara. It is a floral tiara which was given to the Queen Mother by her father the Earl of Strathmore & Kinghorne when she married the then Duke of York in 1923. Strathmore lies partly in Perth & Kinross.

CHAPTER ONE

'See the front o' battle lour'

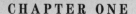

OVER THE CENTURIES, *close to 100 battles, skirmishes and riots took place in Perthshire and Kinross-shire. The more significant, one way or another, include* **METHVEN** *(19th of June 1306),* **DUPPLIN MOOR** *(11th–12th of August 1332),* **KILLIECRANKIE** *(27th of July 1689), and* **DUNKELD** *(21st of August 1689).*

BATTLES, SKIRMISHES & RIOTS

Here are a few others. This is a purely subjective list – two battles and a riot included simply because I find them interesting or quirky in some way. If your curiosity is aroused and you would like to study the subject in more depth, there are some excellent books available on Scottish battles, some of which are included in the Bibliography at the end of this book.

Battle of Mons Graupius

The site of the Battle of Mons Graupius is uncertain, but the Perth & Kinross/Tayside area is certainly one contender, particularly the Gask Ridge near Clathymore, just off the A9 road, near Perth. Other sites lie further north, beyond Perth & Kinross's borders.

The Romans controlled everything from what today is the English border up to Tayside at the time of the battle and there were marching camps close by, so this area is a real possibility.

The only contemporary source describing the battle was written 16 years after it took place, by the Roman historian Tacitus in his biography of his father-in-law Agricola (Roman Governor of Britain at the time). Unfortunately, Tacitus was vague about the location.

The battle took place in AD 83, or AD 84, between the Romans and an alliance of late Iron Age people led by Calgacus, leader of the Caledonians/Picts in the area.

We know his name because he is mentioned by Tacitus in Agricola's biography, but nothing else is known about him.

The Romans had an army of about 11,000 men which included both infantry and cavalry, while the Caledonian army numbered around 30,000. Troop numbers, however, vary according to which interpretation of the battle you are reading. According to Tacitus, the Caledonians lost 10,000 combatants before running away to the hills; the Romans suffered a

loss of only 360 of their men. However, some historians question the veracity of Tacitus's version of events. In fact, some historians are doubtful that the battle took place at all.

Battle of the Clans (North Inch, Perth)

SCOTTISH CLANS have fought numerous battles with each other over the centuries and for a wide variety of reasons, from acquisition of wealth and territory, to perceived slights and even their clan's very survival. Surely one of the oddest was the Battle of the Clans (North Inch, Perth).

The battle is usually portrayed as being between two clans and it depends which account you read as to which clans they were believed to be. Very often Clan Chattan is cited as being one of the antagonists, but Clan Chattan was actually a loose alliance of a dozen different clans which, according to the Clan Chattan Association "originally acted together for mutual security whilst at the same time maintaining their independence". The Association lists the following clans as being members of the group, but in some accounts, one or other of these very clans is claimed to form the opposing side (namely the Mackintoshes and Davidsons):

CLAN CHATTAN

*

Davidson, Farquharson, MacBean, MacGillivray, MacIntyres of Badenoch, Mackintosh, Maclean of Dochgarroch, MacPhail, Macpherson, MacQueens of Strathdearn, Shaw and MacThomas.

*

The battle was fought on the 28th of September 1396 to settle long-standing differences between two rival clans. To modern eyes it could be described as a nasty form of entertainment before an invited audience, in the same way that the Romans enjoyed watching gladiators kill each other.

Robert III had decided that enough was enough in this extended dispute and when his personal representatives were unable to bring matters to a satisfactory conclusion, the two sides were invited to Perth to settle matters once and for all. They were each invited to field 30 men (one account says as few as 12 per side) who were to fight it out to the death.

This was to be a spectator sport, complete with a specially built grandstand for the king, queen and other dignitaries who would attend. The good folk of Perth also gathered on the North Inch to watch the spectacle.

There are some interesting variations to this story. One of them is that one clan's team was a man short, so a local butcher volunteered to make up the numbers. How many died in the battle depends which account you are reading too. Many say that all bar one man died on one side, and that he only escaped by jumping into the River Tay and swimming to the other side.

The death toll varies too. It was 29 lost on one side and all 30 on the other, or 19 and 29, or a solitary survivor on one side and only 10 dead on the other.

Not only was this a battle with a difference, it is also one that is full of contradictions as to who the combatants actually were, how many were involved in the battle and how many survived. However, it provided the inspiration for Sir Walter Scott's book *The Fair Maid of Perth* which he published 432 years later and was a huge success at the time.

Dunkeld Toll Riots

THE EIGHTEENTH AND NINE-TEENTH centuries saw protests all over Britain at having to pay tolls to use new roads and bridges that had been constructed. Wales experienced the 'Rebecca Riots', when farmers disguised themselves in women's clothing and called themselves 'Rebecca and her daughters' (after a biblical reference in Genesis 24:60); they repeatedly tore down toll gates in protest. Perthshire contributed its share of protests at Dunkeld in 1858.

Until 1809, the options for getting to Dunkeld from Perth were either to go a long way around by road or to cross the river by ferry – a dangerous undertaking when the river was in flood. From time to time since AD830 there had been wooden footbridges for the locals to use, but the river had a habit of sweeping them away.

The estimated cost of building a stone bridge was £15,000 and the government agreed to pay half. The other half would be paid by the 4th Duke of Atholl, who owned the land forming the banks the bridge joined. Thomas Telford – nicknamed the 'Colossus of Roads' – had already built 11 bridges by the time he was commissioned to build the one at Dunkeld and went on to build a further 20 afterwards. Needless to say, the cost of the Dunkeld Bridge spiralled, and the duke was faced with a bill for £30,000–£40,000 by the time the bridge was completed. The government initially refused to contribute any more than they had originally agreed to and so a toll was introduced.

Somebody had to pay the excessive cost of its construction; who better than the people who used it? The local populace, who had no option but to use the new bridge to get to church or to reach the new railway station on the opposite bank, were not happy. Even children attending the school at Birnam had to pay a halfpenny for their day return ticket. The populace showed their displeasure by taking a leaf out of the Rebecca Rioters' book and tearing the toll gates down, then flinging them into the river – on several occasions.

Eventually the government increased its contribution to £18,000, the debt was paid off and the toll was finally removed. As for the duke, the matter was still rumbling on in 1872. He was on holiday in London when he found himself summoned to appear before the Queen's Bench. The Mr Robertson mentioned in the action had been strongly opposed to the toll and it would seem he found himself in jail for his trouble, as this piece in the *Teesdale Mercury* of 24th of July 1872 appears to indicate.

THE DUNKELD BRIDGE CASE

THE DUNKELD BRIDGE case has assumed a new appearance altogether. The Duke of Athole, trustee on behalf of the public, having come to London to enjoy the London season, has been pounced upon, and a summons before the Court of Queen's Bench has been taken out against him by Mr Robertson, of Dundonnachie, who is to claim damages from his grace for "wrongous" imprisonment. I understand that the duke can be prosecuted here as well as in Scotland. A committee has been formed in London to push forward the case, and I hear that subscriptions are flowing in.

* * *

The protests against tolls continued into the twenty-first century, with toll bridge charges finally being removed from the Forth Road Bridge and the Tay Road Bridge on the 11th of February 2008 after years of protests and a successful campaign by a local newspaper.

CHAPTER TWO

'But och! It hardens a' within, and petrifies the feeling!'

T HERE ARE MORE than 30 castles in Perth & Kinross. Some of the castles are grand and famous, some remain as the private family homes they were when first built, others are ruined but interesting nonetheless. The seven castles in the Kinross-shire area amount to more castles per head of population than anywhere else in Scotland.

CASTLES, PALACES
and HILLFORTS

Perth Castle

THERE ARE MAGNIFICENT castles to be seen all over Perth & Kinross, including some close to Perth's city centre. Perth had a castle too, once upon a time. Part of the ruins survived until about 1860, but then they were removed and there is nothing at all to be seen of it now.

The castle was built in the twelfth century in an area that was lower than the rest of the city, close to where Perth Concert Hall (Horsecross) is now and was of a motte-and-bailey type construction. Its location was dictated by the need to guard the harbour and river crossing. In fact, it was its location that caused its downfall – quite literally. The River Tay flooded severely in 1209 and swept the whole thing away, along with the bridge. Unfortunately, William I, 'The Lion', was in residence at the time but was saved by some locals. He showed his gratitude by renewing David I's Royal Charter of c.1127 which had bestowed the equivalent of city status on Perth.

With no castle to defend it, Perth was easily captured by forces under Edward I, 'The Hammer of the Scots', in 1298. Defensive walls weren't built until 1304 and, in 1298, Edward's armies only had to contend with ditches. When the city walls were built, a gatehouse, known as the Spey Tower (or Spy Tower), had been incorporated into them near the bottom of South Street. It is said that from there Cardinal David Beaton could watch the execution of people he had condemned as heretics. The tower was demolished in 1766.

Huntingtower Castle

THIS LOOKS TODAY more like the tower house it once was, rather than a castle. Indeed, in the sixteenth century it used to be known as the House of Ruthven, not Huntingtower Castle. It comprises two tower houses, the first built in 1460 and the second some 20 years or so later. It was only in the seventeenth century that they were linked by the central building you see there now. A fifteenth-century painted ceiling and plasterwork in the east tower are among the oldest examples of this type of work in Scotland.

Prior to its acquisition by Historic Scotland, it had been owned by only two families, the Ruthvens and the Murrays. The Ruthvens spent much of their time plotting against James VI. William Ruthven, 1st Earl of Gowrie, had even kidnapped James when the king was 15 years of age and held him prisoner for a year at Ruthven House. When James managed to escape, he had the earl executed and only had him tried for treason after his death. Coincidentally, James's mother, Mary, Queen of Scots, had twice stayed there as a willing guest.

The internationally famous author John Buchan, who was born in Perth, wrote a trilogy of novels featuring a Dickson McCunn as the main character, the first of which was entitled *Huntingtower* (1922). It was adapted as a film, then twice for television and once for radio.

Scone Palace

SCONE PALACE is not a palace. The site where it stands was once a priory, which itself stood on the site of an earlier church. When the priory was granted abbey status, the abbot's quarters then became known as his palace and the label has stuck.

The area has a very long history, being important to both the Picts and the Romans. The Romans were here even before that early church; they camped here in the second century. The site was also of considerable religious significance to the Picts.

Some historians believe the name 'Scone' is of Gaelic origin, others that it comes from the Pictish language.

Scone Palace is a lovely place to visit. Queen Victoria and Prince Albert thought so too when they visited on their way to the Highlands in 1842. I wonder if they were aware that the original medieval village of Scone had been moved 1¼ miles to the east to make way for the new house when it was built early in the nineteenth century – not an unusual practice in those days.

Burleigh Castle

SOMETIMES THE PEOPLE who owned the castles in times gone by were as interesting as the castles

themselves. Burleigh Castle on the outskirts of Milnathort (near Kinross) is one such place and Sir James Balfour, who had married the Burleigh Castle heiress, Margaret, was one such person. He was strongly suspected (both then and now) of being implicated in the murder of Lord Darnley, the husband of Mary, Queen of Scots.

The house in which Darnley was staying belonged to Balfour's brother. Balfour had also purchased a quantity of gunpowder shortly before the house was blown up. He was later made Governor of Edinburgh Castle by James Bothwell, perhaps as a reward for his assistance in the murder. Balfour was a great one for swapping sides if he saw an advantage in it for himself. Mary, Queen of Scots, obviously recognised this when she described him as, "a traitor who offered himself first to one part and then to the other".

Another of Burleigh Castle's infamous occupants was Robert, 4th Lord Balfour, who seems to have inherited his forebear's murderous tendencies. He committed two murders, the first when he was only 12 years old. When a girl's father objected to Robert's amorous moves on his daughter, the boy stabbed him in the heart with a hay fork. Five years later, he killed again. This time he shot the husband of his young sister's governess, with whom he had fallen in love when she was still in his father's employment. His father had sought to thwart this unsuitable affair by sacking the governess and sending his son off to the Continent. But to no avail: Robert made the girl promise to wait for him, swearing that if she married someone else he would kill her husband. When he returned and discovered that the governess had indeed married someone else, despite the promise extracted from her, he carried out his threat. He not only shot the husband, he did so in front of the classful of children the man was teaching at the time. He managed to escape justice for a couple of years, but was then arrested, tried for murder, found guilty and sentenced to death by being beheaded by the Edinburgh guillotine. Again, he escaped, this time with the help of his sister. He took refuge in France but returned in time to join the Jacobite Rising of 1715. When it failed, he was sentenced to death for treason. And yet again he escaped, this time through being given an amnesty. Death finally caught up with him, but from natural causes and not until he was 72 and in his bed at the time.

Cromwell's Citadel

STAND OUTSIDE the Fergusson Gallery in Perth, shut your eyes and imagine it is 1652. You would find yourself standing on top of a bastion, one of four built at each corner of the fortress erected in the city by Oliver Cromwell's army. It covered a huge area, each of its four walls being about 266 feet long. The citadel was big enough to hold 1,000 soldiers and was surrounded by a moat.

As with the other Cromwellian citadels built in Scotland – at Ayr, Inverlochy, Inverness and Leith – the intention was to intimidate the local populace. And in each case, the necessary building materials were acquired by taking what was needed from the city. In Perth, houses were demolished (140 of them), making all those families homeless. None received any kind of compensation and the responsibility for the families' future welfare was placed firmly on the shoulders of the city fathers. The hospital, the grammar school, the stone pillars of the old bridge and even 200 or more tombstones from the Greyfriars Cemetery were utilised, as were the stones from its wall. The North and South Inches contributed soil which was used to build up the ramparts, to give protection against cannon fire.

There were also a number of smaller forts built around Scotland and many of its existing castles were occupied. But castles were not considered to be good defensive positions by then, as their walls could so easily be demolished by artillery.

Whether the sacrifice of so much of the city's various buildings and other structures was worth it is open to debate, as the fort was never tested by being attacked. Then when Cromwell died, Charles II handed it back to the city as compensation for the losses suffered when it was built. The weapons were sold and later so were the building materials. If Perth's inhabitants thought they'd got a fair deal, they were in for a big disappointment. Scarcely had the citadel been demolished and the weapons and stones sold for good prices, than the king changed his mind about gifting it as a present and demanded payment of £366.16.4d (over £28,000 in today's money). As you can imagine, this came as a shock to the local council who wrote to the king pointing out that much of the city had been demolished to provide building materials for the citadel and begging him to change his mind in view of the losses they had already suffered. However, the pleading was to no avail. The reply they received advised them that if they didn't pay up, and pay up promptly, the amount they owed would simply be increased.

If you travel along the old Edinburgh road on your way to Bridge of Earn, you could well be following in the footsteps of the 1,000 citadel soldiers for some of the way. Carry on to Bridge of Earn, turn right just after the Co-operative Society store and Dunbarney School, then follow the road until you have crossed over the railway bridge and taken a sharp left turn. In the field on your left you will see a gnarled old tree that has no leaves, even when other trees are gloriously green. Local legend has it that this is where Cromwell's army camped before its attack on Perth, which is why the tree is today known locally as 'Cromwell's Tree'. Some historians however maintain that Cromwell's Roundheads camped further back, up in the hills where there is now a small army of wind turbines.

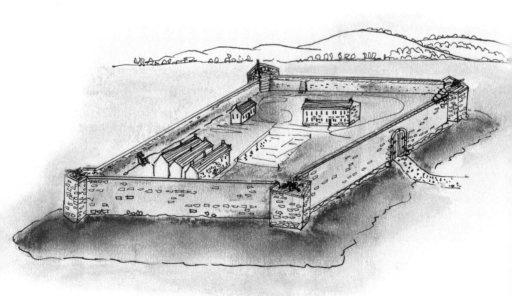

Inchtuthil Fort

THE ROMANS BUILT a fortress at Inchtuthil, which they called Pinnata Castra, long before Cromwell's army got to Scotland. There is nothing much to be seen there today except a few minor earthworks, but in its day, it covered an area of about 50 acres (20 hectares). It was designed to hold about 5,000 men and was intended to be an integral part of Roman efforts to control the north of Scotland. Buildings planned to be inside the walls were the headquarters, officers' houses, barracks, granaries, store sheds, a military hospital, a drill hall and a workshop. Despite its potential importance, it was abandoned between three and five years later, before its construction was even completed. Care was taken to ensure none of the building materials could be used by anyone else. The fort was dismantled when Roman priorities regarding Scotland changed. Even nails were removed and buried. Some of them were found during archaeological excavations, as was pottery which was of a similar date to that found at Pompeii. The Roman army withdrew south and built Hadrian's Wall instead. The site of the fort is on private land southwest of Blairgowrie.

Hillforts

LONG BEFORE any of the beautiful castles in the area, or Cromwell's Citadel, had even been thought of, prehistoric people had constructed their own forts, indicating a population which was gradually becoming more settled. There are 1,694 hillforts in Scotland, which is a large proportion of the 4,147 hillforts identified and mapped in the whole of the UK and Ireland in a recent survey. Some of these are in Perth & Kinross, although they have only survived into modern times as earthworks, on the whole.

Hillforts contained the homes of extended families/tribes or were used as communal meeting places. Sometimes they were only occupied seasonally, rather than permanently. They were located in easily defended positions and surrounded by ramparts and ditches, hence their positioning on top of hills. Hillforts could also sometimes be found between two rivers or on a promontory; the governing factor for a fort's location was ease of defence.

One of the hillforts in the area lies 8 miles north-east of Perth, near the village of Collace. It is on the summit of Dunsinane Hill (1,020 feet) – the same Dunsinane that is mentioned in Shakespeare's play *Macbeth*. There is a small car park at the bottom of the hill and a well-defined path to the hillfort which occupies its summit. Also worth looking for are two cup-marked boulders visible on the south-west side of the fort.

Scotland is also known for the number of vitrified forts within its borders. Vitrification is where the stones in the wall have been subjected to such enormous heat that they take on a glass-like appearance. It is not clear why or how the walls were subjected to this process, although it is felt by some archaeologists that it may have been part of an effort to destroy the fort. It used to be thought that they only occurred in Scotland, but they have also been found in Ireland and some parts of Continental Europe.

The only vitrified fort in the Perth & Kinross area is at Barry Hill, near Alyth, 5 miles north-east of Blairgowrie, where there is a partly vitrified stone wall some 30 feet wide enclosing an area on the summit, although it has been reduced to rubble.

A map showing all the results of the hillfort survey carried out by the universities of Oxford, Edinburgh and University College Cork can be seen at **https://hillforts.arch.ox.ac.uk**. It is possible to zoom right in to see exactly where each hillfort in the UK is located. For those with no access to the internet a physical atlas was made available to buy from the Summer of 2018.

CHAPTER THREE

'They never sought in vain that sought the Lord aright'

Churches and Cathedrals

WHETHER beside a busy street in the middle of Perth or tucked away down a quiet country lane in the middle of nowhere, Perth & Kinross is home to a wide variety of churches. Sadly, some are now derelict and neglected, but there are others which are well worth a visit. I have included the following five because between them they illustrate the old, the more modern, the differences and the surprises.

Dunkeld Cathedral (Dunkeld)

DUNKELD has been an ecclesiastical centre since at least AD 848–9. Some sources put it even earlier at the sixth or early seventh century. It is no accident that Dunkeld Cathedral (dedicated to St Columba) is sited opposite where the River Braan flows into the River Tay as such

St Columba's is a cathedral of two halves. The roofed choir is now home to the local parish church and the unroofed section, although kept in good order, remains a ruin. It took 250 years to build the present cathedral, starting in 1260, with the roofed area being the oldest part. Here, in the east choir, is some of the red sandstone from an even earlier church.

places were thought to be sacred in those early days. So, where better to bring the relics of St Columba to safety from Iona and the constant threat of Viking raiding parties, as it is thought Kenneth MacAlpin (Kenneth I) may have done. During his lifetime, the saint had come here himself to set up a religious centre, so it would be a likely choice. The relics are said to be buried under the chancel steps.

All was not as peaceful as it might have been for this lovely building. Both the Scottish Reformation and the Jacobite Risings saw it sustain damage. Following severe desecration in 1560, when any sign of Catholicism was removed, the chancel was repaired and re-roofed in 1600. Later the building was occupied by the newly commissioned Cameronian Regiment when they took up defensive positions in the cathedral during the Battle of Dunkeld of 21st August 1689. Their orders were to hold on to Dunkeld at all costs. During the sixteen-hour battle the regiment ran out of ammunition. In order to make more required lead, the Cameronian troops stripped it from the roof of the cathedral. When their battle tactics failed in the narrow streets, the Cameronians set fire to the town and burned all but three of the houses.

It is well worth visiting the small Chapter House Museum where there is a permanent local history exhibition. It is free to enter.

St Ninian's Cathedral (Perth)

BY CONTRAST, as cathedrals go, St Ninian's is not very old, having been consecrated in 1850. Nor does it have the soaring towers or spires of many of the medieval cathedrals. An impressive bell tower and spire were originally planned but laying adequate foundations for such structures either proved impossible or were simply too expensive to accomplish. Instead a slender gilded spire known as a flèche graces the roof. The passing traffic either waits at the lights just outside

or drives past with apparent indifference. For all that, it is worth a look inside this Victorian cathedral, the first to be built in Britain after the Reformation – quite an achievement. If you need a break from the hectic world outside its doors, if you seek peace and tranquillity for a while, this is the place to find it. Its architect was William Butterfield, who also designed around 90 other churches.

The majority of sources describe St Ninian as a fourth century missionary who introduced Christianity to Scotland and was the country's first saint. He is even credited with having been trained in Rome. Doubt however has been cast on his very existence by Andrew Breeze, who specialises in the study of Celtic literary texts and oral and written records and has found no trace of Ninian. In a 2014 article by Christopher Howse, Breeze cites Thomas Clancy of Glasgow University who had earlier *"proposed that Ninian was a scribal error for Uinnian"*, meaning that the name of some-one who had actually existed – the sixth-century St Finnian of Moville – had simply been misspelt and then mistakenly taken to be an entirely different person, that is to say St Ninian.

St Mary's Church (Grandtully)

YOU WOULD NOT be surprised to find a beautifully decorated ceiling in a stately home or castle – there's one in Huntingtower Castle, near Perth. It is not the sort of thing you would expect to find in what looks like an old, whitewashed livestock shed located down a minor road off the A827 north-east of Aberfeldy. But this is no shed. It is the six-teenth century chapel of St Mary's and its unprepossessing exterior hides a stunning secret. For part of the ceiling in this little church has been covered with the most exquisite paint-ings. The only other painted church ceiling in Scotland from the same era is in the Skelmorlie Aisle of the remains of St Columba's Church (Largs Old Kirk) in Largs, Ayrshire.

At a time when decoration of any kind was absent from the majority of Scottish churches following the Scottish Reforma-tion, Sir William Stewart decided to have part of St Mary's ceiling painted. Why just part of the ceiling and not all of it is unknown, and the rest of the interior is very plain, although the timber lined barrel-vaulted roof is an attractive feature. Nonetheless, the painted ceiling will doubtless hold all your attention.

The background is filled with fruit, flowers, birds, griffin-type creatures, twirling grape vines and angels. Set in among them are panels of different shapes, sizes and subjects, with the largest in the centre and the others radiating off it and down the wall a little way.

Like many churches, it stands on the site of an earlier one, there being a record of a church at 'Carantuli' in about 1250. The present building was endowed by Sir Alexander Stewart of Grandtully in 1533 and renovated in 1636 by Sir William Stewart.

It is now under the care of Historic Environment Scotland. There is also a graveyard to be explored, which lies to the west of the little church.

St Serf's Church (Dunning)

THIS THIRTEENTH CENTURY former parish church is one of the oldest, most complete medieval parish churches in Scotland. It is also of interest for several other reasons. Before you go inside, stand back and take a moment to admire its imposing Romanesque tower. At about 80 feet high and built of finely dressed blocks of yellow sandstone, it dominates the whole area.

Something to look out for is what appears to be four joined-up eyebrows carved in relief on a stone above the doorway to the church. As the ancient Pictish capital of Forteviot isn't far away, the stone was likely to have been found somewhere near there.

The 'eyebrow' shapes are Neolithic symbols and relate both to clouds and to burials. The worry was that someday clouds might fall down on top of these ancient people. Or they could simply have been placed where they are to carry on the traditional meaning that it was all right to bury people in these grounds.

Evidence from a trench dug by Glasgow University archaeologists suggests that the church stands on the site of what was an earlier monastery. Like so many medieval churches, this one has undergone a few changes over the centuries including an extension that involved the moving of the south wall back by several feet.

Once inside, there are some lovely stained-glass windows to enjoy. Be prepared to be captivated by what stands beneath the tower you so recently admired from the outside. There you will find a masterpiece of Pictish sculpture: the stunning *Dupplin Cross*. Over 1,000 years old, this freestanding cross, 8 feet high, has the name of a ninth century Pictish king carved into it. It portrays a mounted warrior, a man fighting a bear, a wolf and, by complete contrast, a musician playing a harp. It is also decorated with the beautiful swirling patterns so reminiscent of the period.

St John's Kirk (Perth)

THE SCOTTISH REFORMATION began in St John's Kirk on the 11th of May 1559. Following a powerful sermon by John Knox, the congregation stripped the church of anything they considered overly fancy and which reverberated Catholicism. By that stage the mob had the bit between their teeth and stormed off to do the same to Perth's other religious houses. They allowed the monks to take the necessities they needed to live and none of them was attacked or hurt. The several-hundred-strong mob, not all of them from Perth, then denuded the buildings of their Popish trappings but did not damage the fabric of the buildings. It is suggested by some historians that this reaction had been brewing in Perth for a while and that Knox simply provided the catalyst with his sermon.

St John's Kirk is the oldest building in Perth and well worth a visit. At one point, it was divided into three to accommodate three separate congregations, each with its own minister. This was not unusual after the Reformation as congregations were large and frequently split up. Towards the end of the First World War, a committee was formed to organise its restoration to a single church again. To this end, the eminent Scottish architect Sir Robert Lorimer was engaged, and he made a very sympathetic job of it.

There is a lot worthy of your attention in the church, but there is a very simple thing that you could easily miss. As you look down the nave towards the altar there is a large wooden cross hanging down. In the roof are the hooks from which it hangs, and they were made in the fifteenth century.

CHAPTER FOUR

'The boat rocks at the pier'

CRANNOGS

CRANNOGS were built over 2,500 years ago by people who wanted somewhere safe for themselves, their families and livestock to live. In its basic form, a crannog is an artificial island created in a body of water by building up a mound of rocks and timber from the bed of the loch. There are hundreds of them in Scotland. They are also found in Ireland and Wales (a single case), but none in England.

The Scottish Crannog Centre
(Loch Tay)

THE Scottish Crannog Centre at Loch Tay is well worth a visit, especially as a crannog has been reconstructed there using the methods and materials available to prehistoric man as far as was possible. The booklet *The Crannogs of Perthshire*, published jointly by Perth & Kinross Heritage Trust and The Scottish Crannog Centre, gives fascinating detail of just how this was accomplished. Research on crannogs has been carried out on and in Loch Tay since 1979.

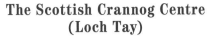

Loch Leven Crannog

ON THE 7TH of September 1887, a crannog was discovered in Loch Leven without the aid of the equipment that is available to the Scottish Trust for Underwater Archaeology today.

Robert Burns Begg, an expert in antiquaries, and incidentally, a great-nephew of Robert Burns, had long believed that Loch Leven had been home to prehistoric residents. One day, he got talking to Richard Kilgour, a boatman on the loch who, since childhood, had been aware of the existence of a pile of stones and timber lying on the loch floor. Kilgour had often wondered what it was. They waited until the water level dropped, as it usually did during summer, and set off to find it. The loch's water level had been reduced anyway, following *"the artificial lowering of its outlet"*. It was not long before they found the mound they were looking for. In his paper on the discovery, Burns Begg reported that when the discovery was notified to Dr Joseph Anderson, the Keeper of the National Museum of Antiquities of Scotland and editor of the *Proceedings of the Society of Antiquaries of Scotland,* he was in for a disappointment. Anderson refused to recognise the structure as a crannog since there was no proof of human habitation.

LUCKILY, due to an exceptionally dry season, the waters of the loch receded to such an extent that in the 2 feet deep water, Burns Begg was able to see that instead of crumbling bit-by-bit, the crannog had collapsed on top of itself. This made it much easier for him to search for the proof he needed to convince Dr Anderson that the Loch Leven pile of stones and timber had indeed been a crannog. Burns Begg was able to recover part of a primitive clay hearth which still had ashes sticking to its surface, charred wood and bits of pottery as well as the wooden handle of what may have been a ladle, plus various animal remains. This provided strong proof indeed that human beings had once lived on this artificial island. Onshore, Burns Begg also traced evidence that a gangway had originally connected the crannog with the land. He was able to work out that on the landward side, part of the 75 feet gangway would have been removable, giving the crannog a bit more security. He surmised that this construction was needed as protection from wild animals, rather than from human enemies, since the crannog was not that far from *terra firma*.

Other Perth & Kinross Crannogs

THE REMAINS OF CRANNOGS are found in several of Perth & Kinross's lochs, some with interesting histories connected to them. Loch Clunie, west of Blairgowrie, has a crannog with a castle on it, which was inhabited right up to the 1960s. It was the birthplace of James Crichton (known as the Admirable Crichton – nothing to do with the 1957 film of the same name). Crichton was born there on the 19th of August 1560 and murdered in Italy just before his 22nd birthday by his girlfriend's jealous ex-lover. Crichton was a child prodigy who had total recall and had also achieved both a bachelor's and a master's degree from St Andrews University by the time he was 14.

Neish Island in Loch Earn is another crannog associated with bloodshed. It was occupied by the Clan Neish from about 1250. There was longstanding bad blood between them and their rivals, the Clan MacNab, who lived on Eilean Ran, an island in the River Lochay at the western end of Loch Tay. It is hardly surprising to learn that when the MacNabs travelled to Crieff in 1612 to buy provisions for their Christmas celebrations, the Neish family waylaid them on their way home and pinched all their goodies. The MacNabs were not happy. In fact, their chief was absolutely livid with rage and encouraged his 12 sons to do something about it. And so, they collected the family's boat from its mooring and between them they carried it for 8 miles over the hills via Glen Tarken to Loch Earn, where they rowed over to the Neish crannog.

BY THIS TIME, the Neish family were having a party, wining and dining on their plunder and having a great time. They had no idea that the MacNab boys were just outside, sinking all their boats. It consequently came as a bit of a shock when 'Smooth John' MacNab hammered on their front door. After they refused to let him in, he simply broke the door down. The MacNabs then piled in and killed all but two of the Neish family. The only ones to escape were a young boy who hid away and a baby girl whose cot was overturned in the turmoil and she lay unnoticed beneath it.

Not content with killing everyone they could find and retrieving their Christmas dinner, the MacNabs cut off the head of the Neish clan chief and took it home as a Christmas present for their father. They carried their boat back as far as Glen Tarken, but then left it there as it slowed them down – bits of it were discovered as late as the nineteenth century.

CHAPTER FIVE

'Do but try to develop his hooks and his crooks'

CURLING AND GOLF

CURLING is thought to be one of the oldest team sports in the world, with the first game – between a monk and an abbot's representative, in Paisley – being recorded in the mid-sixteenth century. According to the records of Paisley Abbey, this took place in February 1541. Curling was certainly being played in the Perthshire area by the end of that century. Even older team sports are hockey, which was mentioned in a proclamation in the fourteenth century by Edward III – although long before that it appeared in Ancient Greek paintings – and polo. Polo is also probably older, having originated in India, China and Iran.

Curling

A CURLING STONE with the date 1511 engraved on it has been found at the bottom of Lake Menteith, which suggests curling was being played in the Perthshire area at least 30 years earlier than in Paisley. Kinross Curling Club is the oldest curling club in the world. It celebrated its 350th anniversary in 2018, so its history stretches back to 1668. Today Kinross Curling Rink hosts 35 clubs. Although the first curling clubs were formed in Scotland, the game is now played in many of the countries that Scots have settled in, wherever the climate is cold enough.

Curling's ice-playing surface is known as a 'sheet' and is usually around 150 feet long and about 15 feet wide. The 'sheet' is covered with tiny droplets of water that become ice. These are known as 'pebbles' and they are the reason the ice is swept once the stone has been sent on its way, because they can cause the stone to 'curl away' from the path it was intended to travel. Hence, the origin of the game's name.

Curling stones are made from granite, with the best quality granite being found on Ailsa Craig in the Firth of Clyde. There are two types:

Blue Hone and Ailsa Craig Common Green. The former is the better quality and has very low water absorption properties, which makes it less susceptible to erosion by the ice. A quarry in Trefor, Wales, also provides granite for curling stones. The Curling stones have specific weight and size limits: the weight must be between 17.24 and 19.96 kilograms, with a maximum circumference of 36 inches and a minimum height of 4.5 inches.

Queen Victoria watched the sport in comfort when she stayed at Scone Palace in 1842. A demonstration was organised for her using the polished floor of the Long Gallery. This led to her agreeing that the Caledonian Curling Club could add the prefix 'Royal' to its name the following year.

In 1924, the first Winter Olympics were held in Chamonix, France. A British men's curling team beat Sweden and France, but it was to be 2006 before the International Olympic Committee retroactively accepted that this was when curling made its Olympic debut. In that same year, it was agreed to include wheelchair curling in the Paralympic Winter Games. The International Olympic Committee granted official medal status to men's and women's curling, to take effect no later than the Olympic Winter Games of 2002, although it had officially agreed to include curling in the programme of the Olympic Winter Games held in Japan in 1998. The sport is governed by the World Curling Federation, whose headquarters are in Perth.

Golf

JAMES IV PURCHASED golf clubs from a bow-maker in Perth in the very early sixteenth century. If golf clubs were being made to a high enough standard for a king to buy them, then the game must already have been played in the area. For surely the king would not have bought them from a rookie club maker? It would seem that golf clubs were being made, alongside bows, arrows and spears, in an already successful Perth business when James IV made his purchase.

> **THE ACCOUNTS OF THE LORD HIGH TREASURER OF SCOTLAND (1502)**
>
> Item, the xxj of September, to the bowar of Sanct Johnestoun [Perth] for clubbes, xiiij s.
>
> Item: the 21st September – to the bow-maker of Saint John's Town [Perth], for golf clubs, 14 shillings.

The game had been played long before James IV bought his golf clubs, because he lifted a long-standing ban on golf which had been imposed by James II in 1457 in order to encourage an increase in archery practice – a far more useful activity than golf during times of war.

Church records show that the game was so popular by the close of the sixteenth century that four parishioners were prosecuted at the Kirk Sessions for playing golf on a Sunday. Nor was this an unusual prosecution. It seems it was a popular sport even back in those far off days.

There were 578 golf clubs in Scotland in 2016, some 30 of which are in Perth & Kinross. These vary from a 9-hole course for use only by guests at a holiday cottage, to the world-famous Gleneagles Golf Club, with its four courses and two nineteenth holes. Some of the holes at the latter even have gloriously Scottish names such as 'Gowden Bestie' for the third; the sixth is 'Mickle Skelp', with 'Wimpling Wyne' the thirteenth.

The most interesting location for a golf club in the Perth & Kinross area is that of the King James VI Golf Club. It is located on an island in the River Tay at Perth and is the only self-contained island course in Scotland. It moved to Moncrieffe Island in 1897. The King James VI course is within walking distance of Perth city centre and, indeed, apart from when the Tay is low enough to allow use of the island's causeway, walking is the only way to get there.

CHAPTER SIX

'An justifies that ill opinion which makes thee startle'

Dragons, Fairies, Ghosts & Witches

SCOTLAND IS STEEPED in tales of the supernatural, so it is hardly surprising that Perth & Kinross has its share of dragons, fairies, ghosts and witches. Here are some of their stories.

Dragons

DRAGONS ONCE ROAMED the Perthshire countryside, bringing death and destruction to its unfortunate inhabitants. Allegedly, that is. There are caves in both Weem Wood, by Aberfeldy, and in the woods on Kinnoull Hill at the edge of Perth, where they were said to live. The latter cave was known as 'the Dragon's Hole' for a very long time and was rediscovered after extensive searching by two determined Perth men. It seems that Sir William Wallace was not bothered about dragons because he is supposed to have used the same cave as a hiding place.

A little over 12 miles south-west of the Kinnoull Hill cave is the quiet Strathearn village of Dunning. It is hard to believe that in the sixth century a dragon was slain there, but according to legend that's exactly what happened, the deed being done by no less a person than a saint. To mark this momentous event, a church was built on the very spot where the dragon met its end and was named after the missionary monk St Serf, who slew the beast. Part of Dunning at Newton of Pitcairn, just south of the village, is known as 'The Dragon' – pronounced 'Drae-gen'.

Nine miles west of Dunkeld is Loch Freuchie where there is a more gruesome dragon story. A young lady called Maidh fancied some rowan berries and asked Fraoch, her boyfriend, to go to get her some. Unfortunately, the rowan tree was on an island where a dragon lived. This did not bother Fraoch, if his love wanted rowan berries, then rowan berries she should have. He managed to avoid the dragon and get the berries. This was not enough for Maidh, oh no. Now, she wanted the tree itself too! So off went Fraoch again, but this time he woke the dragon – maybe he made too much noise digging the tree up. The pair got into a fight and the next morning when Maidh went for a walk she found a grisly sight. Fraoch and the dragon were lying dead on the shore; Fraoch minus his arms and legs which had been chewed off by the dragon before it too died, presumably from a mortal wound received prior to him chomping off Fraoch's limbs.

There is another way of thinking about the whole dragon business though. The old Gaelic word for 'thorn tree' is also 'drae-gen' and is pronounced in the same way as the dragon version. Woods in the sixth century no doubt had their share of thorn trees. So, was there a grove of thorn trees which played an important part in the pagan religion and rituals of the time? And is this what St Serf destroyed in his effort to bring Christianity to the locals? Moreover, was it a thorn tree and not a rowan, that was uprooted in the sad tale of Fraoch and his dragon?

There is a line of thought which suggests that the whole idea of dragons grew from ancient peoples discovering fossils of long-necked dinosaurs such as the Brachiosaurus.

Fairies

DEPENDING ON the weather, sometimes Schiehallion glowers down at you and at others, when the sun is shining, and the mountain's conical summit is reflected in the water of Loch Rannoch, it is considerably more inviting. Who then can blame fairies for making their home in a cave on the lower slopes of the mountain? And why else would the name 'Schiehallion' translate from the Gaelic as 'Fairy Hill of the Caledonians'? The fairies could be helpful to their neighbouring humans too. It is said that they protected the many illicit stills hidden on its slopes from discovery by excise men and that young girls drank from the fairies' well at sunrise on May Day, knowing it would bring them good health and good luck for the coming 12 months.

It seems that fairies did not just favour the 3,553 feet high mountain as home, they quite liked Perthshire's glens too. One of these is Glen Shee whose Gaelic name is 'Gleann Sith', which translates as 'Glen of the Fairies'. There is a standing stone on a hill behind Glen Shee Church, just beyond the graveyard wall – this was the fairies' meeting place. The story goes that in the early 1800s it was planned to rebuild a centuries old Chapel of Ease, but further down the glen. The workmen would turn up each morning to find tools and building materials strewn around all over the place – obviously the work of irritated fairies. Rather than upset the fairies further, the decision was taken to rebuild the church in its original position.

A far less understandable place for fairies to hold their meetings or live is between the M90 and Hatchbank in Kinross. There, today levelled by the plough and hidden beneath the farmer's crops, was a tumulus called 'Fairyknowe'. The fairies must have known that their home would end up near a noisy motorway one day for when the tumulus was investigated in the late eighteenth century, all that was found was an ancient stone coffin with bones and burnt wood within. Not a sign of fairy habitation was found – they must have already moved out.

The Reverend Robert Kirk was born in Aberfoyle (then in Perthshire) in 1644 and produced a book called *The Secret Commonwealth* based on the folklore tales he had gathered about fairies and other mythical creatures. Modern folklore experts consider it to be a very significant work of its kind. The book was reproduced in the nineteenth century by Andrew Lang, who wrote a long introduction and changed its title to *The Secret Commonwealth of Elves, Fauns and Fairies*, to suit perhaps the more romantic, thistledown viewpoint of fairies of his Victorian audience.

According to the stories Kirk gathered, fairies were far from the sweet, helpful creatures described earlier. People strongly believed in both their existence and their frequent malevolence. For instance, fairies thought nothing of stealing a healthy newborn baby to keep for themselves and replacing it with a sickly child of their own. And, in another tale, a baby's mother didn't die, she had simply been abducted to act as a wet nurse for one of their fairy babies.

Kirk either died in 1692 or, as many of his parishioners firmly believed, he was snatched by fairies for daring to give away their secrets in his book.

Ghosts

IT IS HARDLY surprising to have reports of ghosts being seen after a battle and the Battle of Killiecrankie, fought just north of Pitlochry on the 27th of July 1689, was a particularly bloody engagement. About 2,000 men died there including the Jacobite leader, John Graham of Claverhouse, better known as 'Bonnie Dundee'. In fact, Dundee seems to have had a prophetic dream the night before the battle. He was half asleep when he saw a man with blood pouring from a head wound standing by his bed. Three times this happened, and three times Dundee went back to sleep, despite the apparition pointing towards Killiecrankie and saying he would meet Dundee there. As indeed he did, in a manner of speaking, although Dundee died from a bullet wound in his side, not his head.

Elliott O'Donnell published a book, *Scottish Ghost Stories*, in 1912 and recorded a frightening

story recounted to him by the lady the incident had terrified. The lady was cycling through the glen and decided to camp by the roadside. She woke up at two in the morning to the sound of distant gunfire that seemed to be getting closer. She then saw a Highlander running wildly towards her. Things just got worse and worse after that, with troops marching towards her and grue-some dead and wounded bodies scattered around. As if that was not enough to contend with, a young woman appeared and began plundering the bodies, killing anyone who was still alive.

Dead bodies lying around, as well as marching soldiers have been seen in broad daylight on other occasions too, particularly around the battle's anniversary, as has a red glow over the battleground. The A9 road was recently widened in the area where the battle took place, but nothing exciting was seen or found on the archaeological investigations that took place prior to the roadworks commencing.

Unrequited love accounts for quite a few ghosts, most of them young women, some of which are considered next.

Castle Huntly might be an open prison now, but there has been a castle on the site since the twelfth century, occupied by a ghost since the 1600s. The young lady in question was a member of the Lyon family who owned the castle at the time. She fell in love with one of the servants, but her family were having none of it. They locked her in her room. She either fell, or was pushed, out of her bedroom window and was dead when she was found on the ground outside. There is another, much more modern ghost that is also said to haunt the castle and this time it is a young man.

George Paterson bought the castle from the Lyons in 1777. The second ghost is one of his descendants who died 162 years later. Richard was the only son of Colonel Adrian Paterson and he died tragically in a boating accident on the River Tay in 1939. Despite his aquatic demise, his ghost has only been seen in the bedroom of the lovelorn young lady, whereas she wanders round the grounds.

Huntingtower Castle on the outskirts of Perth also has a young female ghost who floats around the castle and grounds – usually around dusk. She is Dorothea, daughter of the 1st Earl of Gowrie and she also fell in love with one of the servants. Dorothea and her boyfriend had a narrow escape when her suspicious mother very nearly caught them together in the servants' side of the castle, but Dorothea escaped by safely leaping from the servants' tower to the family tower and snuggling down in her own bed, which is where her mother found her. The couple eloped the very next day. Dorothea presumably returned because she remembered her happy secret love trysts there.

The derelict village of Lawers sits in the woods beside Loch Tay and is a scheduled monument. Derelict it may be, but the ghost of Lady Lawers still considers it her home. She was reputed to predict events in the area, which all came true except three, which remain unfulfilled – so far. She is still seen from time to time, so if you fancy a spot of ghost hunting over a weekend, there is a nice hotel in the neighbouring hamlet just up the road where you can stay.

Not all ghosts are human.

On the A93 north of Blairgowrie the apparition of a ghostly dog has perturbed many a canine pet and also upset passing horses.

Witches

DESPITE THE FACT that Scotland had only roughly a quarter of the population of England in the seventeenth century, it put three times as many people on trial for witchcraft – somewhere between 4,000 and 6,000 people, mostly from the Lowlands. Although there were more acquittals than was usual in England, the most common punishment was first to be strangled, then burned. The last trial was in the early eighteenth century.

At Blair Atholl there is a 'Witch's Rock' where women who were thought to be witches were thrown off it into the waters below. As in so many watery judgments, the innocent drowned and the guilty did not – only to receive more permanent punishment some other way.

Not only can the Strathearn village of Dunning claim its own dragon, but it has a witch's memorial too. About a mile to the west of the village, on the B8062, sits a big cairn of stones with a cross atop it. In white paint beneath the cross it says: *"Maggie Wall burnt here 1657 as a Witch"*. But was she?

Certainly, there were many accusations of witchcraft in the Strathearn area, particularly in the mid-seventeenth century. Six of those accused were actually from Dunning, but none of the six was called Maggie Wall. Various researchers have failed to find any evidence that she even existed, let alone that the poor woman met such a ghastly end. And yet, the painted legend is kept fresh and clean, so someone believes it to be true. Visitors still stop to have a look at it – as did the murderers Myra Hindley and Ian Brady back in the 1960s.

Both locals and visitors tend to assume that Maggie Wall was a real person – why else, they ask, would there be a monument to her? The truth, however, is far stranger. The archaeology of the structure's stonework suggests a very late eighteenth-century or very early nineteenth-century date, long after the witchcraft era ended. In addition, the original estate maps and factor's books of the era show that in 1755 the site where the monument now stands was a walled field named 'Maggie's Walls' – which is to say, the 'walled field of Maggie'.

If you might be tempted to think that at the very least there must have been a woman named Maggie, you are to be disappointed there as well: several eighteenth-century written records refer to the field as 'Muggies Walls' – 'Muggie' is an obscure word, but it may be related to 'Mugg' and 'Mugg-ewe', "*a sheep with a good coat of wool*". This is the discomfiting truth: 'Maggie Wall' is not the name of a person, it is a place name.

Another witch who may not have actually existed is Kate McNiven. Some accounts have her being burnt to death, others have her being rolled down a hill in a barrel and then being burnt to death. She had been a nurse to the Graham family of Inchbrackie and one of the proofs that she was indeed a witch was that she had the ability to turn herself into a bee. It was claimed she buzzed around the head of her employer, the laird. However, no record of a trial for anyone of this name can be found, and where and when she was burned to death varies from one account to another.

Some people were actually recorded as going on trial for witchcraft. A memorial to 11 of these unfortunates (one a man) has been created by Lord Moncrieff in the grounds of Tullibole Castle in Crook of Devon. The 11 were tried and found guilty in 1662. The memorial to them takes the form of a circular maze consisting of 2,000 beech trees. At the centre of the maze is a stone pillar with the names of all the victims carved on it.

CHAPTER SEVEN

'Tis but a pang, and then a thrill'

FAIR MAID OF PERTH

PERTH OWES A LOT to Sir Walter Scott's
novel *The Fair Maid of Perth*. Indeed, early in the first chapter
he writes, *"Perth, so eminent for the beauty of its situation,
is a place of great antiquity"*.
Perth is referred to as 'The Fair City' over 100 times in his book
and the city has described itself thus ever since.

THE STORY MIXES real and imagined events and characters and is set at the end of the fourteenth century. Scott was initially inspired by the true story of the Battle of North Inch and included it as part of the storyline. He developed a plot revolving around Henry Gow's attempts to win the love of Catharine Glover, a glove maker's daughter. But she also attracted the attention of a rival for her affections in the person of the Duke of Rothesay. The action-packed story includes an attempted abduction of Catharine and lots of fighting and bloodshed, which incorporates, but is not limited to, the Battle of the Clans (North Inch, Perth). In the end Henry gets the girl.

Sitting on a bench near the Tourist Information Office in Perth's High Street is a bronze sculpture of the 'Fair Maid'. It was made by Graham Ibbeson in 1995, who also sculpted the statue of Eric Morecambe that stands on the promenade in Morecambe, Lancashire.

Georges Bizet is best known for his opera *Carmen*, but Scott's book also inspired him to compose the music for *La jolie fille de Perth*, an opera in four acts. It didn't prove to be terribly popular at the time and has not been performed very often since, but the whole opera can be found online. It is slightly over two-and-a-half hours long and was commissioned by the Théatre Lyrique in Paris as a follow-up to *The Pearl Fishers*.

La jolie fille de Perth was first performed there on the 26th of December 1867. The story bears little resemblance to Scott's book and Catharine's character has been changed, however Bizet cannot be blamed for that as the libretto was written by Jules-Henri Vernoy de Saint-Georges and Jules Adenis. A live performance of the Serenade from the opera (in English from a 1949 recording sung by Richard Lewis and conducted by Sir Thomas Beecham) can also be found online.

Two films were produced in the 1920s which were based on *The Fair Maid of Perth* including a feature film in 1923 starring Dame Sybil Thorndike's brother Russell as Dwinning. Although he appeared in 10 films, Russell Thorndike's first love was writing, and he penned 15 books, including the *Dr Syn* series.

There was also a short film of Scott's book which was released in December 1926. It was produced by Miles Mander. He returned to Britain in 1918 after spending a few years in New Zealand. As well as becoming a novelist, playwright and film exhibitor, Mander was an actor, appearing in three different versions of the film *The Three Musketeers*, playing a different role in each of them. He bore a remarkable resemblance to Field Marshall Montgomery and had he not been too tall, would have been recruited as Monty's double.

The Fair Maid's House, which is located in Curfew Row (behind Perth Concert Hall), is now occupied by the Royal Scottish Geographical Society and has been since 2011. As well as housing the society's regional office, it is also a public visitor and education centre. There is an 'Earth Room', an 'Education Room' and an 'Explorers' Room', each with an absorbing approach to such subjects as maps, explorers, our own planet as seen from outer space and other subjects of very wide geographical interest. At the time of writing, its opening hours are 1.00 pm to 4.30 pm, Thursdays to Saturdays between April and October. Groups can request a special visit at other times.

The Fair Maid's House is thought to be the oldest secular building in Perth, with part of it dating from 1475. The Glover Incorporation owned the building, on and off, from the early seventeenth century to the late nineteenth century. I wonder if this is why Scott decided to make the occupation of the Fair Maid's father a glove maker and their surname Glover, since the house would have been in the possession of The Glover Incorporation when Scott stayed overnight in Perth in 1793. Although nobody is sure where he stayed, some accounts suggest

it was at one of two nearby hostelries – The Salutation Hotel or The George Hotel (today the Royal George). Wherever it was, that may have been when Scott got to know of the house – but that is sheer speculation on my part.

William Topaz McGonagall is considered, by most people, to be an appalling poet. That did not stop him writing over 250 poems or performing them before audiences. In 1864, he moved to what he called 'a garret' in Perth's South Street where he lived for eight months. So, it is hardly surprising that The Fair Maid's House did not escape the McGonagall treatment, nor was he bothered about getting his facts right. For example, the third verse of his poem about the place states, *"King James the First of Scotland was murdered there"*. No, he was not. James was assassinated while he was staying at Blackfriars Monastery, and by a group of conspirators, not robbers. Although the poem rambles on for nine verses, only the first three are included here.

THE FAIR MAID OF PERTH'S HOUSE

All ye good people, afar and near,
To my request pray lend an ear;
I advise you all without delay to go
And see the Fair Maid's House - it is a rare show.
Some of the chairs there are very grand,
They have been cut and carved by a skilful hand;
And kings, perchance, if the truth were told,
Have sat on them in days of old.
King James the First of Scotland was murdered there,
And his cries for mercy rent the air.
But the Highland robbers only laughed at him,
And murdered him in the dungeon and thought it no sin.

CHAPTER EIGHT

'Contented wi' little and cantie wi' mair'

FAMOUS PEOPLE

Some very well-known people have been born
in the Perth & Kinross area, others were visitors,
and some have chosen to live here.
Here are a few of them.

HISTORICAL

ALEXANDER KINMOND BELL (1868-1942)

PERTH & KINROSS'S MAIN LIBRARY is named after Arthur Kinmond Bell, whose father established the company that made Bell's whisky. A. K. Bell, as he was known, was presented with the Freedom of Perth on the 18th of March 1938 in *"acknowledgement and recognition of the many benevolent and public services rendered by him to his Native City, more particularly in the maintenance and development of industry of the City, the provision of housing accommodation and of facilities for the recreation of the Citizens and in testimony of the high respect and esteem in which he is held by the Magistrates, Council and Citizens"*. Bell founded the Gannochy Trust to further his philanthropic ideas and to improve life for those less fortunate than himself. Initially, his generosity was for the benefit of the people of Perth but was later extended to cover the whole of Scotland.

The Trust's philanthropic ventures cover a wide range of projects, from donations to small charities, to building sheltered housing, to providing cricket pitches and a woodland park. The River Tay is now clean and usable for water sports thanks to various sewage schemes funded by the Gannochy Trust.

* * *

ALEXANDER BUCHAN (1829-1907)

DR ALEXANDER BUCHAN, LLD, FRS, FRSE was born in Kinnesswood, Kinross. He became an eminent meteorologist after whom 'Buchan Spells' were named because he was the first to take note of them. 'Buchan Spells' are departures from the normally expected temperature occurring during certain seasons. Buchan also created the weather map as the basis of modern weather forecasting.

JOHN BUCHAN (1875-1940)

JOHN BUCHAN was born at 20 York Place, Perth, in August 1875 and is best known for his novel *The Thirty-Nine Steps*, his seventeenth published work, which first appeared in 1915. It has since been produced as a film on several occasions and as television, stage and radio plays, none of which have been true to his book. Buchan was a prolific writer all his life and published more than 30 novels, as well as half-a-dozen collections of short stories, and some 100 other works, including history and biographical books, some being published before he had even left university. Buchan was created 1st Baron Tweedsmuir GCMG, GCVO, CH, PC in 1935. He led a very full life: after graduating from Oxford, he became (in alphabetical rather than chronological order) an author, barrister, historian, journalist, military intelligence officer, an MP and publisher. Buchan later served as Governor General of Canada, from 1935 until his death five years later.

DAVID DOUGLAS (1799-1834)

PERTHSHIRE BOTANIST DAVID DOUGLAS introduced over 200 plants to Britain including the Douglas Fir (which was named after him), lupins and mahonia. Born at Scone, Douglas left school aged 11, but when he was given access to the substantial botany library of Sir Robert Peston, for whom he worked as a gardener, he took full advantage of the opportunity and studied the books well. His next job was in the Botanical Gardens at the University of Glasgow where the Professor of Botany, Sir William Hooker, recognised his potential and the two mounted a number of botanical expeditions together. Sadly, Douglas met an untimely end when in the Sandwich Islands (today known as the Hawaiian Islands), he fell into an animal pit used to capture wild bulls. It was not the fall that killed him – it was the wild bull that joined him and gored him to death very shortly afterwards.

ROBERT DOUGLAS (1859-1929)

PHILANTHROPIST ROBERT DOUGLAS was born and raised in Scone. There he learned from his father, who owned the local jam factory, how to make jam on a commercial scale. He and his brother later emigrated to America where they used their knowledge to develop a new method of extracting pectin from apples and thereby made a fortune selling it under the brand name 'Certo'. They increased their fortune when they sold the brand to General Foods Corporation of America.

Douglas specified in his will that a proportion of his estate *"should be devoted in perpetuity for the benefit of the people of New Scone and the vicinity, and to the betterment of living conditions in the village"* and that a trust should be set up in his home village to administer it. His wishes were carried out and a new school was built, as was the Robert Douglas Memorial Home and Cottages. In addition, Scone's public hall was extended and a new wing, named after him, was added to Perth Royal Infirmary.

NIEL GOW (1727-1807)

NIEL GOW WAS A SELF-TAUGHT MUSICIAN who grew up in Inver, near Dunkeld. He became famous throughout Scotland, performing all over the country. Gow's method and style of playing the violin became the accepted way to do it and is still followed today. There is a nice little video online of Yehudi Menuhin playing Gow's composition of a *Lament on the Death of his Second Wife*, as a tribute to him.

ROBERT KIRK (1644-1692)

THE REVEREND ROBERT KIRK was born in Aberfoyle (then in Perthshire). He wrote a book called *The Secret Commonwealth* based on the folklore tales he had gathered about fairies and other mythical creatures. Modern experts consider it to be a very important work on the subject of folklore. Kirk also spent some time in London helping to translate the *Bible* into Gaelic. He died in 1692.

WILLIAM McGREGOR (1846-1911)

THE FOUNDER OF THE ENGLISH FOOTBALL LEAGUE was a Scotsman! He was William McGregor, who was born in Braco, a hamlet near Dunblane. He was 23 when he moved to Birmingham and seven years later was invited to join the committee of Aston Villa

Football Club, which had only been formed five years before. It was McGregor's idea to form a professional league and Aston Villa became one of the 12 founding members of the Football League which had been created by him. He was its first chairman and then its president.

FELIX MENDELSSOHN (1809-1847)

ANOTHER FAMOUS MUSICIAN was a visitor to the county. The composer Mendelssohn visited Black Linn Falls at The Hermitage, Dunkeld, in 1829. (A 'linn' is the pool below a waterfall.)

ELIZA OGILVY (1822-1912)

ELIZA OGILVY WAS A WELL-KNOWN POET in her time, the quality of her work even being compared favourably by some with Lord Byron's poems. Like so many of her cultural contemporaries, her name faded out of the public consciousness and now her main claim to fame is her longstanding friendship with fellow poet Elizabeth Barrett Browning. Depending on source, Eliza was born in Perth, various places in India or Devon. She certainly lived in Perth for a time; one of the letters sent to her by Elizabeth was forwarded on to her from that city. The two women met when they lived in the same building in Florence and when Ogilvy and her husband returned to England, the two poets corresponded until Browning's death in 1861. In a letter to Ogilvy dated 1854, Browning showed a sense of humour when she wrote, *"We are all poets in Florence. Not to rhyme would be a distinction"*.

PONTIUS PILATE (d. AD38)

ACCORDING TO LEGEND, PONTIUS PILATE was a Perthshire lad, born in the village of Fortingall, near Glen Lyon. Around AD83, a Roman diplomat arrived in Scotland to undertake negotiations with Metallanus, a leader of the Picts. While he was here, the diplomat married a local woman and they had a son who returned to Rome with his father and eventually became the fifth prefect of the Roman province of Judaea. He is, of course, notorious today for his part in the trial and crucifixion of Jesus. The legend of Pilate's birth in the county was well established by the Middle Ages and appeared in *Holinshed's Chronicles* (published in 1577). Other legends have Pilate born in Spain and Germany, as well as Central Italy, but very little is actually known about his early life, so we might as well believe him to have been born in Perthshire.

BEATRIX POTTER (1866-1943)

A NOTABLE LITERARY VISITOR to Perthshire was Beatrix Potter. The Potter family home was in London, but from the time she was five years of age each summer for the next 11 years was spent at Dalguise House, 8 miles north of Dunkeld. These days, the house is used as an outdoor activity centre.

It was during these holidays that Potter's interest in nature was encouraged by the local postman, Charles Mackintosh. He was a postman all his life, but also became a very well-known naturalist in his own right. Potter developed a particular interest in fungi during her visits here and, in fact, became something of an expert. Her drawings were so accurate that the mycologist W. P. K. Findlay included many of her drawings in his 1967 book *Wayside & Woodland Fungi.*

On her last visit, Potter wrote two 'picture letters' to her ex-governess's children about Peter Rabbit in Mr. McGregor's garden and Jeremy Fisher's fishing trip. These letters are thought to have formed the basis for two of the 28 children's books she went on to write – *The Tale of Peter Rabbit*, published in 1902 and *The Tale of Mr Jeremy Fisher*, published in 1906. *The Tale of Mrs Tiggywinkle*, published in 1905, is thought to have been based on the washerwoman at Dalguise.

Beatrix Potter's books have been translated into over 35 languages and sold more than a 100 million copies. There is a garden and interactive exhibition dedicated to her life at Birnam Arts & Conference Centre.

JOHN RUSKIN (1819-1900)

JOHN RUSKIN WAS A MULTI-SKILLED MAN whose expertise included art criticism, art patronage and draughtsmanship. He was also a watercolourist, a prominent social thinker and philanthropist. Ruskin was married to Effie Gray at Bowerswell House, Perth in April 1848. Gray's father had bought Bowerswell House, near Kinnoull Hill, from Ruskin's father.

In a notorious love triangle, Gray claimed her marriage to Ruskin was never consummated and got the marriage annulled. She then married Ruskin's protégé, the Pre-Raphaelite painter John Everett Millais – in the drawing room of her father's home. For a while, the couple lived at Annat Lodge, by Bowerswell House.

* * *

WALTER SCOTT (1771-1832)

SIR WALTER SCOTT WAS A PROLIFIC WRITER, producing poetry, plays, short stories and non-fiction, as well as 21 novels between 1814 and 1832. He is considered to have invented the genre of the 'historical novel'. Scott's day job was Clerk of Session and Sheriff-Depute of Selkirkshire. He never lived in the Perth & Kinross area, but did pass through Perth in 1786 and in 1793 when he stayed overnight in the city; and again in 1796. Scott used his memories of these journeys when writing *The Fair Maid of Perth,* published over 30 years after his last trip.

Scott Street in Perth is named after him and there is a life-sized statue of the great writer on the Marshall Place side of the South Inch, opposite King Street. Scott was an honorary member of the Perth Literary & Antiquarian Society. When he died in September 1832, the Literary Society opened a subscription to raise money to provide a memorial to the author in the form of a statue, which originally stood at the bottom of High Street. It was later acquired by the Town Council and moved to its present South Inch location. The Literary Society had money left over after they had paid for the statue, so they commissioned the sculptor John Steell to make a white marble bust of the author. There is a video online which portrays the bust very favourably.

Incidentally, John Steell was also responsible for the statue of Scott at the base of the Scott Monument in Edinburgh.

WILLIAM SOUTAR (1898-1943)

AT 32, POET WILLIAM SOUTAR had already been bed-ridden for two years with ankylosing spondylitis (arthritis of the spine) when he penned the words, *"My life's purpose is to write poetry"*. Born in Perth in 1898 and educated there, Soutar joined the navy when he left school in 1916 and was demobbed in 1919, when his illness was already beginning to make itself felt. Despite this, he attended Edinburgh University where he was awarded a third-class degree. Soutar's early poetry used pretentious language and was not deemed to be particularly good. However, his parents adopted his orphaned cousin in 1927, which may have prompted him to start writing poetry for children in the local Perth dialect. It is certainly felt that his poetry gradually started to improve once he wrote it in Scots, as well as English.

Among Soutar's many visitors during his bed-ridden period in an extended lower-floor room in his parents' Wilson Street home were two eminent, but contentious poets – Ezra Pound and Hugh MacDiarmid.

Soutar shared the latter's vision of reviving Scottish literature but tended to have a more 'native' and local language approach to his work than that of MacDiarmid.

Soutar was not only a poet, but a diarist of note, having kept a diary since he was 21. He even kept it during the last months of his life when he was suffering from tuberculosis, as well as his original illness. Soutar was only 45 when he died in 1943. His *Diary of a Dying Man* is considered to be of major importance both within his own canon of work and that of Scottish literature.

Controversial as usual, fellow poet Hugh MacDiarmid edited *Soutar's Collected Poems,* but failed to include many of his friend's most outstanding works.

ROBERT LOUIS STEVENSON (1850-1894)

ROBERT LOUIS STEVENSON, author of *Treasure Island, Kidnapped* and *The Strange Case of Dr Jekyll and Mr Hyde*, among numerous other books, was an inveterate traveller. He journeyed through Europe, America and the South Pacific, where he died in Samoa. Because of ill health, he also spent a couple of months in Kinnaird Cottage at Moulin, near Pitlochry. While Stevenson was in residence, he wrote *Thrawn Janet, The Merry Men* and *The Bodysnatcher*. The cottage is still there.

J. M. W. TURNER (1775-1851)

THE ARTIST J. M. W. TURNER came to Scotland in 1801 producing several pieces of work when he was in the Pitlochry area. He returned a little over 30 years later when he was asked to illustrate Walter Scott's collected *Poetical Works*: he was commissioned to produce 24 designs at 25 guineas each. While he was in Kinross-shire, Turner made a couple of sketches of Loch Leven Castle and another of Burleigh Castle, at Milnathort, although they were not part of his Scott commission.

JULES VERNE (1828-1905)

LITERARY GIANT JULES VERNE and his wife came to Scotland in 1859 and visited Callendar while they were here. Although the town is now in the council area of Stirling, at the time of Verne's visit, it was located in Perthshire.

* * *

WILLIAM WORDSWORTH (1770-1850) and SAMUEL TAYLOR COLERIDGE (1772-1834)

THE POETS WILLIAM WORDSWORTH AND SAMUEL TAYLOR COLERIDGE travelled extensively in Scotland with Wordsworth's wife and sister in 1803, visiting Black Linn Falls at The Hermitage, Dunkeld. Altogether, their travels took them on a journey of over 600 miles, most of it on an uncomfortable one-horse open carriage. They did manage to meet up with Walter Scott while they were here, though missed seeing Robert Burns's widow.

MODERN ENTERTAINMENT

ALAN CUMMING (b.1965)

ACTOR ALAN CUMMING OBE won his award for services to film, theatre and the arts and for his work as a gay rights campaigner. Born in Aberfeldy and now living in the USA, Cumming has appeared in numerous films, television shows and plays. He has an honorary Doctor of Arts degree from the University of Abertay, Dundee. He is also a patron of the Scottish Youth Theatre.

FRED MACAULAY (b.1956)

PERTH-BORN COMEDIAN FRED MACAULAY started his working life in accountancy, before he became a professional comedian at the age of 31. He was the first ever Scottish compere at the Comedy Store in London. He is a regular at the Edinburgh Fringe and many comedy festivals worldwide, as well as making numerous appearances on various Radio 4 comedy panel shows. MacAulay has an MA in Accountancy and Jurisprudence from the University of Dundee, as well as an honorary Doctorate awarded to him in 2006 in appreciation of his time there as Rector.

DOUGIE MACLEAN

DOUGIE MACLEAN, OBE, born in Dunblane, is an award-winning singer-songwriter of international fame and whose songs have been covered by many artists. His music also featured in the film *The Last of the Mohicans*. MacLean received his OBE *"in recognition of his contribution to music and charity"*.

EWAN McGREGOR (b.1971)

EWAN MCGREGOR, OBE, is a Scottish actor who was born in Perth and raised in Crieff, where he went to school. His first professional role was in a television series, *Lipstick on Your Collar*. The film *Trainspotting* in 1996 gave McGregor his big international break-through and three years later he starred as a young Obi-Wan Kenobi in *Star Wars: Episode I – The Phantom Menace*. McGregor has appeared in numerous films, as well as on television and the stage, and been a UNICEF UK Ambassador since 2004. UNICEF states that *"Ewan actively supports our work during emergencies and continues to tirelessly fundraise and advocate for UNICEF's work for children worldwide"*.

MODERN SPORTS

CARLY BOOTH (b.1992)

CARLY BOOTH, BORN IN COMRIE, is a professional golfer who became the youngest ladies' club champion in Britain at the age of 11.

EILIDH CHILD (b.1987)

COMMONWEALTH, WORLD AND EUROPEAN 400 metres hurdles medallist Eilidh Child was born in Perth.

GEMMA FAY (b.1981)

GEMMA FAY who was born in Perth, is an international football goal-keeper. At the time of writing, she plays in Iceland and has made some 200 appearances for the Scotland national team – its most capped player.

EVE MUIRHEAD (b.1990)

EVE MUIRHEAD led the Scottish curling team to a bronze medal in the 2014 Winter Olympics in Sochi, after winning the European Championships in Moscow in 2011. Born in Perth, Eve is based in Pitlochry.

CHAPTER NINE

'But pleasures are like poppies spread'

FESTIVALS

As well as various agricultural shows and Highland games, there are all sorts of festivals and activities going on in Perth & Kinross throughout the year. Here are just a few of them. The list is correct at the time of writing but check before you go that the event is still on.

JANUARY

Flambeaux Parade, Comrie: When Big Ben chimes midnight on New Year's Eve, that's the signal for Comrie's Flambeaux Parade to begin. Tarred rags are tightly bound to the ends of long, thick birch poles, lit and paraded around the village. A pipe band leads the parade and folk in fancy dress bring up the rear. Once prizes have been awarded to the fancy dressers, the torches are thrown into the River Earn to signify casting out evil spirits.

Burns Night: Robert Burns's birthday is celebrated all over Perth & Kinross (and indeed the world) on the 25th of January every year.

FEBRUARY

Winter Words Festival, Pitlochry: A book festival described by its organisers as, *"an engaging range of genres and themes in this festival celebration of the written and spoken word"*.

MARCH

Clay Pigeon Shooting, Killiecrankie: All year round at Highland Fling Bungee, c/o The National Trust for Scotland, Killiecrankie Visitor Centre, Killiecrankie.

APRIL

Salmon Fishing: The salmon fishing season in Scotland runs from early February until late October on most salmon rivers.

MAY

Perth Festival of the Arts, Perth: Perth Festival of the Arts: *"An annual 10-day May Festival with opera, choral, drama, dance, rock, folk music and visual art. One of the longest running independent arts festivals in Scotland."*

Spring Watch Safari, Aberfeldy: Highland Safaris: *"Capture the magic of the Highlands and enjoy the early morning wildlife".*

JUNE

Solas Festival of Arts & Ideas, Blackruthven by Tibbermore, near Perth: Solas: *"Solas brings performers and thinkers together to entertain, surprise and delight; a rich Midsummer celebration of art and ideas".*

Midsummer Music Evening, Kenmore, near Aberfeldy Scottish Crannog Centre: *"Midsummer magic featuring Scottish music around a log fire. ... Pop, Rock and Contemporary".*

Cream O' The Croft, Abernethy: Comrie Croft: *"A family-friendly festival of camping and fun activities for all ages, or a weekend of mountain bike racing and partying ... or both".*

Words of War Book Festival, Black Watch Museum, Perth: A book festival described by its organisers, the Black Watch Museum and Tippermuir Books, as *"concentrating on books – fact, fiction, drama, and poetry – of wartime stories, peace and conflict, war and culture (art, poetry, and film), the military, weaponry, and military history."*

JULY

Rewind Festival, Scone Palace, near Perth: Rewind: *"We handpick all our acts to make your weekend an 80s extravaganza".*

AUGUST

Blairgowrie Rugby & Ales Festival, JJ Coupar Park, Blairgowrie: Blairgowrie Rugby Club: *"10 a-side rugby tournament accompanied by a fine selection of Ales and plenty of activities for kids and family".*

SEPTEMBER
Perth Festival of Yarn, Dewars Centre, Glover Street, Perth:
Festival of Yarn: *"Over 60 amazing vendors catering for all fibre enthusiasts".*

OCTOBER
The Crieff and Strathearn Drovers' Tryst, Faskally Wood near Pitlochry:
Drovers' Tryst: *"One of Scotland's premier walking festivals. It celebrates the cattle drovers who made Crieff one of the most important places in Scotland in the 1700s, when the Crieff Tryst was the largest cattle market in the land".*

The Enchanted Forest, Around Crieff: Enchanted Forest:
"The Enchanted Forest is Scotland's premier sound and light event."

NOVEMBER
Kinross Winter Festival, Kinross: Kinross-shire Local Events Organisation: *"November and December in Kinross-shire is bursting with music, family activities, local talent and community spirit. The annual Winter Festival brings together community groups, local businesses and Kinross-shire Local Events Organisation (KLEO) to present a wealth of events for all tastes".*

DECEMBER
St Andrew's Day Scottish Festival, Perth: St Andrew's Day Festival:
"Live music and a marketplace selling food and drink from Scotland's natural larder".

LOCATIONS THAT HAVE BEEN USED FOR FILMS INCLUDE:

CHARIOTS OF FIRE (1981)

This Oscar winning film features a brief scene shot in Crieff; it shows Liddell awarding prizes at a Highland Games ceremony. Eric Liddell took part in the 1924 Summer Olympics in Paris and his best distance was the 100 metres. Unluckily, the heats were to be run on a Sunday, and his strong Christian beliefs precluded him taking part. Instead, Liddell ran in the 400 metres which was held on a weekday and he won gold.

EDGE OF DARKNESS (1985)

This television drama serial starring Bob Peck included scenes shot at Gleneagles.

ROB ROY (1995)

Starring Liam Neeson, Jessica Lange and Tim Roth, some scenes in *Rob Roy* were filmed at Loch Leven and some at the fifteenth-century Megginch Castle in the Carse of Gowrie.

MRS BROWN (1997)

Taymouth Castle, in the Highlands, near Loch Tay, stood in for the royal residence of Balmoral Castle. The original Taymouth Castle was demolished in the early nineteenth century to make way for the present, much larger neo-gothic building, which is now a 6-star hotel.

THE BRUCE (1996)

Historic Scotland rates Drummond Castle, near Crieff, as, *"the best example of formal terraced*

gardens in Scotland". It was used as a location for both this film and *Man to Man* (2005).

AARZOO (1999)

This Bollywood musical, mostly filmed in India, includes a few scenes filmed around some of Perth's statues.

YOUNG ADAM (2003)

Starring Crieff's own Ewan McGregor and also Tilda Swinton, included in this film were scenes shot in Perth's Sheriff Court.

LES LIAISONS DANGEREUSES (2003)

This mini-series was based on the classic eighteenth-century novel *Les Liaisons Dangereuses* by Pierre Choderlos de Laclos and starred Catherine Deneuve and Rupert Everett. Some of it was shot in the Perth & Kinross area.

ON A CLEAR DAY (2005)

The plot of this film revolves round a redundant shipyard engineer's plan to swim the English Channel. Scenes showing him and his friends training for their epic swim were filmed at Loch Monzievaird, near Crieff.

THE DESCENT (2009)

Even though the action in this horror film is supposed to take place in the Appalachian Mountains in North America, the white-water rafting in the opening shots was filmed at the Linn of Tummel, near Pitlochry. Other outdoor scenes were shot near Dunkeld. The follow-up, *The Descent Part II* was filmed entirely in the south of England.

TEZZ (2012)

Part of this Bollywood blockbuster was filmed in Perth.

*

BELLE (2013)

Even though no part of this film was shot in Scotland, never mind Perth & Kinross, it is mentioned here for two reasons. First, Didi Elizabeth Belle, the subject of the film, lived at Scone Palace. Second, an eighteenth-century painting within the palace, of Belle and her cousin Lady Elizabeth Murray, inspired the film's writer to create the screenplay.

This true story takes place in the eighteenth century and is about the mixed-race daughter of a naval officer, Sir John Lindsay. Her great-uncle, the 1st Earl of Mansfield, raised her alongside his niece at Scone Palace.

THE RAILWAY MAN (2013)

Starring Colin Firth and Nicole Kidman, some of this film was shot in Perth's lovely old Victorian railway station.

OUTLANDER (2014+)

Adapted from the gripping bestselling historical time travel series of novels by Diana Gabaldon, the TV series *Outlander* was filmed in locations in England, Prague and Cape Town as well as various parts of Scotland, including Perth & Kinross.

The magnificent wild landscape of Rannoch Moor appeared in Series 1. In Episode 11 of the same series, Tibbermore Church,

just 4 miles west of Perth was the scene for the witch trial; the film company spent eight days in the church filming. Drummond Castle Gardens, near Crieff, with its finely trimmed topiary shrubs and hedges, doubled nicely for the grounds of the Palace of Versailles in Season 2 of the show.

TIME TEENS: THE BEGINNING (2015)

Originally a television series, although this fantasy time-travel film is set at the 'headquarters of the World Time forum in Perth', only one small scene was actually filmed in Perth; that was shot in a tearoom on the city's High Street.

CHAPTER ELEVEN

'The birth-place of valour, the country of worth'

GALLANTRY AND THE VICTORIA CROSS

THE VICTORIA CROSS (VC) is the highest decoration of the United Kingdom honours system. It is awarded for gallantry *"in the face of the enemy"* to members of the British armed forces. The VC can be awarded to civilians if they are *"serving with the armed forces"* – to date, only five have been bestowed on civilians (four in the Indian Rebellion of 1857-8 and one in Afghanistan in 1879).

Before the VC, the highest award for gallantry was the Order of the Bath, but it could only be given to senior officers. To balance things out a bit, the Distinguished Conduct Medal was created in 1854 for NCOs and privates. Other countries had medals for gallantry regardless of rank. The idea that Britain should have one too came from Liberal MP and former naval officer, Captain Thomas Scobell, in December 1854 and the Duke of Newcastle, the then Secretary of State for War, who in January 1855 announced the creation of a new medal for *"a signal act of valour in the presence of the enemy"*. Both Queen Victoria and Prince Albert were actively involved in the decoration's establishment. Indeed, it was Prince Albert who changed the name of the medal from 'The Military Order of Victoria' to 'The Victoria Cross'.

The Queen took particular interest in the design of the medal and suggested reducing its size slightly from that shown in the original design. She also changed the slogan on the front of the medal. Originally it was *"For the Brave"*, but she felt that implied that anyone who was not awarded the VC, wasn't brave. Consequently, she changed it to *"For Valour"*. In addition, she changed the medal material from copper to bronze.

Victoria also made it clear that she wished to personally present as many of the medals as possible and chose the 26th of June 1857 to do so for the first time. She also decided to stay on horseback while she performed the ceremony for the first 62 recipients of the new medal.

At the time of writing, 1,358 VCs have been awarded, three of them being awarded twice to the same men. The following men from Perth & Kinross have received the VC.

WILLIAM DAVIDSON BISSETT VC

Citation:

"On 25 October 1918 east of Maing, France, Lieutenant Bissett was commanding a platoon, but owing to casualties took command of the company and handled it with great skill when an enemy counter-attack turned his left flank. Realising the danger he withdrew to the railway, but the enemy continued to advance and when the ammunition was exhausted Lieutenant Bissett mounted the railway embankment under heavy fire and, calling for a bayonet charge, drove back the enemy with heavy loss and again charged forward, establishing the line and saving a critical situation".

JAMES CRAIG VC

Citation:

"For having volunteered, and personally collected other volunteers, to go out under a heavy fire of grape and small arms, on the night of the 6th September 1855, when in the right advanced sap, in front of the Redan, to look for Captain Buckley, Scots Fusilier Guards, who was supposed to be wounded. Serjeant Craig brought in, with the assistance of a Drummer, the body of that Officer, whom he found dead, in the performance of which act he was wounded".

(A 'Redan' is an arrow-shaped embankment forming part of a fortification and, along with the date, would indicate that this James Craig's action took place at the Siege of Sebastopol during the Crimean War of 1853-6.)

* * *

JOHN MANSON CRAIG VC
Citation:

"For most conspicuous bravery on the occasion of an advanced post being rushed by a large party of the enemy. This officer immediately organised a rescue party, and the enemy was tracked over broken country back to his trenches. Second Lieutenant Craig then set his party to work removing the dead and wounded. During the course of this operation his men came under heavy rifle and machine gun fire. A NCO was wounded, and the Medical Officer who went out to give aid was also severely wounded. Second Lieutenant Craig at once went to their assistance and succeeded in taking the NCO under cover. He then returned for the Medical Officer, and whilst taking him to shelter was himself wounded. Nevertheless, showing great perseverance, he succeeded in rescuing him also. As the enemy continued a heavy fire and in addition turned on shrapnel and high explosives, Second Lieutenant Craig scooped cover for the wounded and thus was the means of saving their lives. These latter acts of bravery occurred in broad daylight, under full observation of the enemy and within close range. On three previous occasions this officer has behaved in a conspicuously brave manner, and has shown an exceptional example of courage and resource".

(This action took place on the 5th of June 1917 during John Craig's service in Gaza, Egypt.)

JAMES PALMER HUFFAM VC
Citation:

"For most conspicuous bravery and devotion to duty on the 31st Aug., 1918. With three men he rushed an enemy machine-gun post and put it out of action. His post was then heavily attacked and he withdrew fighting, carrying back a wounded comrade. Again on the night of 31st Aug., 1918 at St Servin's Farm, accompanied by two men only, he rushed an enemy machine-gun, capturing eight prisoners and enabling the advance to continue. Throughout the whole of the fighting from Aug. 29th to Sept. 1st, 1918, he showed the utmost gallantry".

PETER LEITCH VC
Citation:

"For conspicuous gallantry in the assault on the Redan, when, after approaching it with the leading ladders, he formed a caponier across the ditch, as well as a ramp, by fearlessly tearing down gabions from the parapet, and placing and filling them until he was disabled from wounds".

(This action took place on the 18th of June 1855 during the Siege of Sebastopol.)

WILLIAM GEORGE DRUMMOND STEWART VC
Citation:

"For distinguished personal gallantry at Lucknow, on the 16th November 1857, in leading an attack upon and capturing two guns, by which the position of the mess house was secured".

GEORGE THOMPSON VC
Citation:

"Flight Sergeant Thompson was the wireless operator in an aircraft which attacked the Dortmund-Ems Canal by daylight on 1st January, 1945. Just after releasing its bombs, the aircraft was hit by a heavy shell which set it on fire and caused extensive damage. Flight Sergeant Thompson without hesitation went through the fire and exploding ammunition and rescued the gunners from the mid-upper and rear gun-turrets, both of whom were unconscious. With his bare hands he extinguished their burning clothing. He then with great difficulty made his way back through the burning fuselage to report to the captain of the aircraft. He might have devoted his efforts to quelling the fire, but preferred to go through it to save his comrades, hazarding his life. Three weeks later he died of his injuries. One of the gunners he rescued survived; he owes his life to the gallantry of Flight Sergeant Thompson, whose courage and self-sacrifice will ever be an inspiration to the Service".

(This action took place over the Dortmund-Ems Canal, Germany.)

* * *

WILLIAM JOHN VOUSDEN VC CB

Citation:

"For the exceptional gallantry displayed by him on the 14th December, 1879, on the Koh Asmai Heights, near Kabul, in charging, with a small party, into the centre of the line of the retreating Kohistani force, by whom they were greatly outnumbered, and who did their utmost to close round them. After rapidly charging through and through the enemy, backwards and forwards, several times, they swept off round the opposite side of the village and joined the rest of the Troop".

CHAPTER TWELVE

'When drinkers drink'

HISTORIC PUBS, INNS AND HOTELS

MANY OF THE HOTELS, INNS AND PUBS IN PERTH & KINROSS HAVE HISTORY ATTACHED TO THEM. HERE ARE JUST A FEW EXAMPLES.

Balgedie Toll Tavern, Kinross

IN THE SIXTEENTH CENTURY, travellers would have had to stop at the Balgedie Toll Tavern to pay the toll that was due. It is a much bigger building now than it was in 1534, the actual toll house having been incorporated into the present building.

Birchwood Hotel, Pitlochry

A FORMER VICTORIAN FAMILY home built in 1875, Birchwood is today a lovely country house hotel.

Crieff Hydro, Crieff

IN 1868, DR THOMAS MEIKLE founded the Strathearn Hydropathic Establishment at a cost of £30,000, specifically to practise the 'science' of hydropathy. This is a system of treating illness using water both internally and externally. It was invented in the 1820s by Vincent Priessnitz who had treated Dr Meikle in Austria.

Meikle was contemptuous of some of the treatments Priessnitz promoted, due to his own training as a proper medical doctor (which Priessnitz certainly wasn't). This was an era when spa towns such as Cheltenham, Bath and Harrogate were flourishing in England; maybe the temptation to cash in on the craze was also a tempting factor. Meikle's establishment was built with the intention of attracting a well-heeled clientele and was an immediate success.

During the Second World War, Crieff Hydro was used to house Free Polish forces. These days, it operates as a popular spa hotel.

Cromlix House, Kinbuck

THIS 5-STAR HOTEL is a Victorian mansion 4 miles north of Dunblane. It used to be in Perthshire before boundary changes gave it to Stirlingshire. Originally built in 1874 as a family residence, the house burnt down four years later. The building which stands there now was constructed in 1880 and later operated as an hotel. It is now owned by the tennis player Andy Murray.

The hotel itself may not be that old, but records show that in the 1500s the Bishop of Dunblane sold the lands which constitute Cromlix to his brother.

* * *

Dalmunzie Castle, Glenshee

LOCATED IN THE HEART of Glenshee, the original Dalmunzie Castle dated back to 1510 and stood on the south bank of the burn. By the eighteenth century, it had fallen into disrepair and in the nineteenth, Dr Charles Hills Macintosh, the 10th Laird of Dalmunzie, built a hunting lodge on the opposite bank, but retained the castle's name. This is the building that became the present-day hotel.

Kenmore Hotel, Kenmore

SCOTLAND'S OLDEST INN, the Kenmore Hotel, was built in 1572 and is located at the eastern end of Loch Tay, 6 miles west of Aberfeldy on the A827. The tiny modern village of Kenmore in which it is located is thought to stand on the site of an earlier medieval village, so it may be that the hotel is a surviving remnant of that era. The Earl of Breadalbane is responsible for building the lovely village you see today, constructed at some time after 1755. It might be surmised that his motivation was to provide homes for the villagers whose houses may well have been knocked down so that Taymouth Castle could be built. Moving whole villages to a more convenient location was not at all unusual on either side of the border at that time. In fact, it is what happened when Scone Palace was built too.

King James Pub and Kitchen, Perth

ALTHOUGH THE King James Pub (formerly Christie's Bar) is modern, there is a possibility that the remains of the medieval Blackfriars Monastery lie beneath it. If so, keep a weather eye open for a royal ghost, because that is where James I was assassinated in 1437.

Meikleour Arms, Meikleour

THE CONSERVATION VILLAGE of Meikleour is home to this small country hotel and pub built in 1820. It is owned and run by Meikleour Estate, which remains a family business many centuries after it was founded by French settlers. The estate has been held by the same family for centuries, through various turbulent times on both sides of the Channel. Even today, the estate's management has dual nationality.

* * *

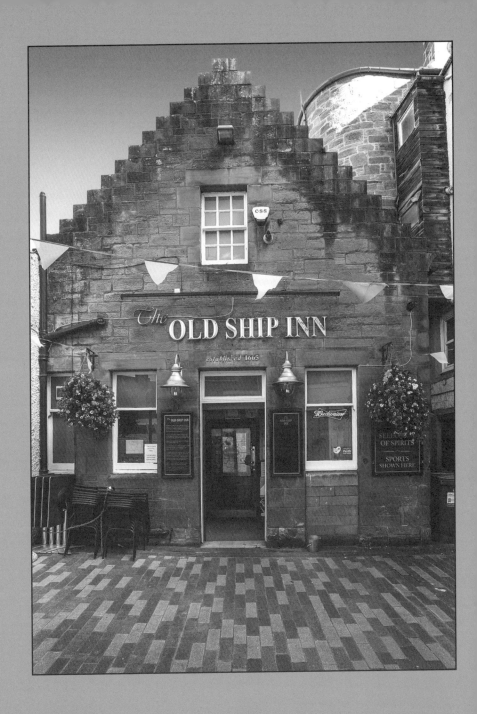

Mercure Perth Hotel, Perth

THIS FORMER FIFTEENTH-CENTURY watermill maintains its connection to its origins in a lovely old stone building. There are glass portholes in the Mercure Hotel's lounge bar, enabling you to watch the water which still trickles along the lade that powered the original water wheel.

Moulin Inn, Pitlochry

FIFTY YEARS BEFORE the Jacobite Rising of 1745, the Moulin Inn was already up and running. There were two rooms on the ground floor, with two rooms above that and two further rooms on the floor above those. One of the upper rooms was used as a meeting place by the local elders, who dealt with neighbourhood squabbles and minor crimes.

Old Ship Inn, Perth

THE OLD SHIP is the oldest pub in Perth; its name has remained unchanged throughout its history, according to records which date back to 1665. It is, however, thought that its existence goes back even further and that it provided a welcome haven for sailors as far back as medieval times.

The name was significant because at one time the harbour was just at the bottom of the road. So, sailors did not have far to stagger back to their ship after a drunken night in the pub.

Royal Dunkeld Hotel, Dunkeld

LOCATED ON ATHOLL STREET, in the 'Gateway to the Highlands' town, the Royal Dunkeld Hotel, a former coaching inn, was built at the beginning of the nineteenth century.

Struan Inn, Calvine, Pitlochry

BUILT IN 1863, this inn was intended to be patronised by travellers arriving at the nearby Struan Railway Station, which closed to both passengers and goods traffic on the 3rd of May 1965.

CHAPTER THIRTEEN

'And a' the comfort we're to get'

HOSPITALS

During the medieval period
it is estimated that between
160 and 170 hospitals were built
in Scotland, thirteen of them
in Perth & Kinross.

HOSPITALS THESE DAYS are for people with health problems, but in medieval times they also cared for orphans, housed the poor and gave food and shelter to travellers. There were even specialist hospitals, for example, some dedicated themselves to the care of lepers, such as St Leonard's in St Andrews. In all likelihood there was a leper hospital in Dunkeld too, as the hospital there was called St George, whose name was often used for leper hospitals in Scandinavia; it was also the only Scottish hospital to use that saint's name.

Some mediaeval physicians thought leprosy was due to tainted blood, resulting in various treatments designed to purify it. One such treatment was a mixture containing gold; it was thought that drinking it would cleanse the blood and restore the body's humours. Other 'cures' included regular bloodletting, administration of a drug made with viper's flesh and other ingredients, or medication using mercury – which was often incorporated into various medical therapies. But the treatment most frequently prescribed was isolation, even from one's family.

There was a hospital at Scotlandwell, a village at the eastern end of Loch Leven. Medieval hospitals were run by various religious orders and the one at Scotlandwell was no exception. It belonged to the Red Friars (Trinitarians) which was an order founded in the twelfth century.

Historically the word 'spital' (sometimes spelt 'spittel') meant a hospital for those with contagious diseases, such as leprosy. So, places with the word 'spital' in their name would seem to indicate that a hospital existed there in the past. Spittalfield, a village about 6 miles from Dunkeld, is one such place.

More recent times have seen further hospitals established and then either disappear or change function.

Murray Royal Hospital

THE CITY'S PSYCHIATRIC HOSPITAL first opened in 1827. It was closed and some of the old buildings demolished in 2012. Construction of new facilities began in June 2010 and a new hospital was opened in 2013.

Perth Royal Infirmary

DISPENSARIES served a similar purpose to modern outpatient clinics and one was established in Perth in the early 1830s. Dispensaries were often the forerunners of hospitals, as proved to be the case here with Perth Royal Infirmary. The original hospital building, then known as Perth City & County Infirmary, was constructed in 1836-8 following a generous gift of £1,000 in 1836; and its Grecian architectural style was designed to impress. That building is now home to the A. K. Bell Library, after acting first as a Red Cross hospital, before hosting Perth County Council offices for at least 50 years and finally becoming a library in 1991.

Perth Royal Infirmary was opened by George V and Queen Mary on the 10th of July 1914. Later additions to the original building include a maternity block in 1975, a care of the elderly unit in 1981 and a new ward block in 1993 that included an A&E department.

Cottage hospitals, now commonly called community hospitals, are a great resource in local areas.

Aberfeldy Community Hospital

ABERFELDY'S ORIGINAL COTTAGE HOSPITAL, known as 'The Home', opened in 1879. The present building opened in 1910, the land the building stands on being donated free by the Marquis of Breadalbane. The hospital was extended in the 1920s and became part of the National Health Service when it was formed in 1948. The hospital, including its boundary walls and gate piers, are listed buildings, albeit only category C.

Blairgowrie Community Hospital

£2,643 WAS THE PRICE PAID to have this former cottage hospital built in 1901. An operating theatre and x-ray facilities were opened in the early 1960s, followed by a new GP unit in 2014.

Crieff Community Hospital

CRIEFF'S FIRST HOSPITAL was built in 1906 and was closed 90 years later. It was replaced by a new hospital in a different location in 1995.

Pitlochry Community Hospital

THIS WAS FORMERLY KNOWN as Irvine Memorial Nursing Home and was built in 1901 as, *"a memorial to Dr William Stewart Irvine, a medical practitioner who had practised in the district for nearly 60 years"*.

* * *

ONE LAST HOSPITAL DESERVES TO BE MENTIONED, even though it is no longer a hospital, because its history began with James VI.

In 1429, James I founded the first and only Carthusian Monastery in Scotland for a prior and 12 monks. It was destroyed in 1559 following the Reformation, but in 1587 James VI confirmed an earlier Royal Charter which had been granted by his regent when the king was younger. Its function was to raise revenue to be used on behalf of the burgh's poor. The building was intended to be a home for the poor, a school and an infirmary to care for the sick. One hundred years later, the original building was demolished by Cromwellian troops to provide building material for the citadel built on the South Inch.

The present building was constructed in 1749-50 at a cost of slightly over £1,600 (£246,700 today). It was converted into 21 flats in 1974-5 and is still administered by officials of St John's Kirk and Letham St Mark's Church, who are known as 'Managers', and are overseen by an official whose title is 'Hospital Master'. The rents provide an income to continue the original function of the Hospital, as described above.

As James I and his wife were both buried at the Carthusian Monastery, I imagine they are still there somewhere. There is a noticeboard outside the flats giving lots of information about the place; it mentions that the couple are buried there, but not where. The search for the grave locations is the subject of current archaeological investigation.

CHAPTER FOURTEEN

'Come, Firm Resolve, take thou the van'

INNERPEFFRAY LIBRARY

THE CONCEPT OF LIBRARIES IS AS OLD AS THE HILLS.

*The idea of a library lending books freely
to anyone who wants to read them is not.
The oldest free public lending library in Great Britain
is Cheltham's Library in Manchester which was
established in 1655. In Scotland, the oldest
is to be found in the little hamlet of
Innerpeffray, near Crieff.*

THERE HAD BEEN PLENTY of subscription and private libraries established all across Britain much earlier than Cheltham's, some of them still in existence. However, the idea of lending books to the general public for nothing was seen as being fraught with danger. It was felt that people would borrow them, but never bring them back. This turned out not to be the case. For instance, over a four-year period in the mid-nineteenth century, a free public lending library in Liverpool issued some 700,000 books of which only six were not returned.

However, 200 years earlier, around 1680, David Drummond, 3rd Lord Madertie, also felt he could trust the general public. He had grown tired of the violence that had beset Scotland for decades. He decided to take no further part in it, but instead devote his time to collecting books, reading them and writing. Aware that the general population in Scotland was now mostly literate, he made the decision to allow them access to the books he had gathered for his own reading pleasure.

Furthermore, he wanted that access to be free of charge *"for the improvement and education of the population particularly the young students"*. He wished to make sure that access to his library would be free in perpetuity, and to that end left 5,000 Scottish Merks to enable his successors to ensure it was. (A Merk was a Scottish silver coin, and back then one Merk was a week's wages for a skilled tradesman.) One of these coins would have bought you at least half-a-dozen large copper kettles, or 33 kilograms of bacon or 1,000 bricks. So, the money left by David Drummond was a considerable amount at the time. Unfortunately, it was not enough to cover costs for the more than 300 years that his library was to last and these days visitors and fundraising have to provide the funds needed.

Over the years more books were added to the collection, so that the original stock of 400 books has grown to 5,000. Among the many subjects they cover are law, music, poetry, politics, gardening, witchcraft, animals, farming, medicine and European history. The books date from the sixteenth century to modern editions. There is even the library's 'Borrowers' Ledger', which is a record of everyone who ever borrowed a book from this wonderful collection. It provides an interesting social insight into who made use of this facility.

Originally the books were housed in the chapel, which is so

close to the present library that only a few inches separate the gables of the two buildings. Today David Drummond's books are housed in a Georgian property which was used from 1762. It was designed by Charles Freebairn, an Edinburgh architect. The library no longer lends books out and ceased lending them in 1968 but remains open to the public several days a week from March to October each year.

The chapel where the books were originally stored is still there. It is open to visitors from the 1st of April to the 30th of September from 9.30am to 5.30pm, except on Mondays and Tuesdays. The Drummond family worshipped there and kept up their Catholic faith's practices even after the Scottish Reformation. They may have got away with it because the chapel was used as a family mausoleum. It was originally a private chantry chapel with four priests, who would have been employed to pray for the souls of deceased Drummond family members, thus speeding their way through purgatory and onwards to heaven. It also contains a splendid monument carved by John Faichney in 1707, which is well worth seeing despite the very sad reason for its existence. It commemorates John's wife and the ten children who pre-deceased her.

CHAPTER FIFTEEN

'Princes and Lords are but the breath of kings'

LORD-LIEUTENANTS

"LORD-LIEUTENANTS ARE APPOINTED BY THE QUEEN, ON THE ADVICE OF THE PRIME MINISTER FOR EACH COUNTY OF ENGLAND AND WALES, AND IN SCOTLAND, ON THE ADVICE OF THE FIRST MINISTER FOR EACH AREA OF SCOTLAND, SAVE FOR THE CITIES OF ABERDEEN, DUNDEE, EDINBURGH AND GLASGOW, WHERE THE LORD PROVOSTS ARE EX OFFICIO LORD-LIEUTENANTS.

THE LORD-LIEUTENANT'S ROLE IS, LIKE THE MONARCH'S, ESSENTIALLY NON-POLITICAL AND SEEKS TO PROMOTE A SPIRIT OF CO-OPERATION BY ENCOURAGEMENT OF THE VOLUNTARY SERVICES AND BENEVOLENT ORGANISATIONS, AND BY TAKING AN ACTIVE INTEREST IN THE BUSINESS, INDUSTRIAL AND SOCIAL LIFE OF THE AREA."

This is a list of people who served as Lord-Lieutenant of Perthshire.

(The office was replaced by the Lord-Lieutenant of Perth & Kinross in 1975.)

JOHN MURRAY, 4th Duke of Atholl
17th March 1794 – 29th September 1830

THOMAS HAY-DRUMMOND, 11th Earl of Kinnoull
18th October 1830 – 18th February 1866

GEORGE KINNAIRD, 9th Lord Kinnaird
26th February 1866 – 7th January 1878

JOHN STEWART-MURRAY, 7th Duke of Atholl
9th February 1878 – 20th January 1917

JOHN STEWART-MURRAY, 8th Duke of Atholl
15th March 1917 – 15th March 1942

KENNETH KINNAIRD, 12th Lord Kinnaird,
28th April 1942 – before 30th April 1960

MUNGO MURRAY, 7th Earl of Mansfield and Mansfield
30th April 1960 – 2nd September 1971

DAVID HENRY BUTTER, 25th November 1971 – 1975
Butter became Lord-Lieutenant of Perth & Kinross in 1975.

The present incumbent is
BRIGADIER MELVILLE S. JAMESON CBE,
who was appointed in 2006.

This is a list of people who have served as Lord-Lieutenant of Kinross-shire.

(The office was replaced by the Lord-Lieutenant of Perth & Kinross in 1975.)

GEORGE GRAHAM, 17th March 1794 – 18th December 1801

WILLIAM ADAM, 30th January 1802 – 17th February 1839

SIR CHARLES ADAM, 28th March 1839 – 16th September 1853

SIR GRAHAM GRAHAM-MONTGOMERY, 3rd Baronet,
7th August 1854 – 2nd June 1901

HENRY JAMES MONCREIFF, 2nd Baron Moncreiff,
18th July 1901 – 3rd March 1909

SIR CHARLES ADAM, 1st Baronet,
26th March 1909 – before 9th November 1911

JOHN JAMES MOUBRAY, 9th November 1911 – 21st October 1928

ALEXANDER PRICE HAIG,
6th December 1928 – before 8th March 1934

SIR HENRY PURVIS-RUSSELL-MONTGOMERY, 7th Baronet,
8th March 1934 – before 9th March 1937

JAMES AVON CLYDE, LORD CLYDE,
9th March 1937 – 16th June 1944

HENRY KEITH PURVIS-RUSSELL-MONTGOMERY,
9th October 1944 – 1st October 1954

CHARLES KEITH ADAM, 15th January 1955 – before 27th May 1966

ROBERT CHRISTIE STEWART,
27th May 1966 – before the 12th June 1974

SIR DAVID HENRY BUTTER, 12th June 1974-1975

CHAPTER SIXTEEN

'My heart's in the Highlands, wherever I go'

MUNROS, CORBETTS, GRAHAMS, DONALDS AND MARILYNS

KNOWN AFFECTIONATELY as the 'Matterhorn of Perthshire', at 3,553 feet Schiehallion is a Munro. Like the Matterhorn, Schiehallion has a conical shape; unlike the Matterhorn, Schiehallion is easy to climb or walk up.

The idea to list all Scotland's peaks over 3,000 feet came from the then editor of the Scottish Mountaineering Club's journal in 1891. Lists of Scotland's major mountains had already been compiled, but none of them were useful for the serious mountain climber. A mountaineer himself, Sir Hugh Munro's reputation for meticulous attention to detail made him the obvious choice to undertake the task. The very first peak he recorded was Ben Lawers, in Perthshire. Although it is only the tenth highest of all the Scottish Munros it is, however, the highest mountain in the Southern Highlands and a very popular peak. The lowest of the Perthshire Munros is Meall a'Choire Leith at 3,038 feet. There are 282 Munros to ascend, 27 of them in Perthshire.

Munro regarded his first list as incomplete and expected to add to it. Sadly, he died of pneumonia in 1919 aged 63, never having climbed all the 3,000 feet peaks himself. And, he was right to consider it incomplete: four further modifications were added to the list during the course of the twentieth century.

THEN THERE ARE Corbetts, Grahams, Donalds and Marilyns. There are 221 Corbetts in Scotland, 21 of them in Perthshire, the highest being Beinn Nan Oighreag at 2,982 feet. Corbetts are peaks between 2,500-3,000 feet with a drop on all sides of 500 feet.

J. Rooke Corbett, after whom these hills are named, was the first Englishman to complete all the Munros in 1930. This Bristol-based climber compiled the list of Corbetts in the 1920s, but it was only published after his death in 1949.

There are 223 Grahams, 14 of them in Perthshire, the highest being Shee of Ardtainaig at 2,490 feet. Grahams have to have a height of 2,000 feet. Their drop on all sides has to be 490 feet. Grahams initially had a less elegant name – they were known as the 'Elsies' ('LCs', short for 'Lesser Corbetts') in a list first published by Alan Dawson in *The Relative Hills of Britain*. At more or less the same time, Fiona Torbet (née Graham) also published a similar list. The mountains were later named after her.

Donalds number 89 in Scotland with only two in Perthshire. Their height should be the same as the Grahams, but they only need 98 feet of surrounding drop. The list was compiled by Percy Donald and is maintained by the Scottish Mountaineering Club.

Marilyns were so named as a nod towards the Munros and the film star. About every other hill higher than 492 feet above their surrounding land is classified as a Marilyn and their numbers throughout the UK run into the thousands. There are 573 of them in Scotland which are lower than 2,000 feet, 27 of which are in Perthshire.

CHAPTER SEVENTEEN

*'Auld nature swears, the lovely dears
her noblest work she classes'*

NATURE
RESERVES

There are 43 national
nature reserves in Scotland,
three of them in Perth & Kinross.
The sort of things you'll find in
them vary, from the remnants of
ancient pine forests, to a wide variety
of birds, animals, plant life and
even an important area of
peat conservation.

NINE THOUSAND YEARS AGO, the first pine trees arrived where Abernethy Forest stands now; the trees you walk through today have descended from those very first arrivals. The forest also shelters a variety of birds including the largest of the grouse family, the capercaillie. At the time of writing, the National Park Authority and Scottish Natural Heritage are researching a way to comply with a legal requirement to find how the public can view this protected bird, which does not impact on it in a negative way. Capercaillies go to forest paths to eat the grit on them as it helps them digest their food. Authorities suggest that sticking to the footpaths is therefore the best way to see them. There is a super little 2¾-minute film on YouTube narrated by David Attenborough entitled 'The Capercaillie Bird Defends its Territory'. It shows capercaillies displaying during the mating season and one of the males attacking Attenborough – and winning.

There are also ospreys to be seen at the RSPB's Loch Garten Osprey Centre. It is open every day, 10.00am to 6.00pm, from the 1st of April to the first weekend in September. You can also watch a live webcam of activity at an osprey nest at the Scottish Wildlife Trust's Loch of the Lowes location.

If you are really lucky you might see a pine marten too. They were known to be in the region and their range has continued to expand throughout Perth & Kinross. In fact, one of them almost scuppered the building of a multi-million-pound housing development near Scone when it was spotted in the woods there in 2016. These animals are legally protected.

One part of the ancient forest area, near Nethy Bridge, is known as Dell Woods and it has areas of bog woodland which support many specialist and rare species of plants. There are over 200 varieties of vascular plants here (land plants that have woody tissues for conducting water and minerals) as well as some insectivorous plants, such as round-leaved sundew and butterwort. Most of the pines you see around you here will be between 100 and 140 years old, with a few of them over 200 years old. Do not be fooled by the short, stubby pines you see growing in boggy areas. They number some of the oldest trees in the wood among them, but they have simply found themselves growing in an area of very poor nutrition, and so are unable to reach for the sky like their taller, more noticeable colleagues.

There are also some throwbacks to the Ice Age in the form of a single colony of twinflower, all growing from the same plant. They are so called because each stem carries two pink bell-like flowers. In addition, there are several hundred spikes of creeping lady's-tresses, a pretty little multi-flowered white orchid. It is almost exclusively found in Scotland, mainly in remnants of Caledonian forest, such as the one described here. Much less attractive, but endangered nevertheless, is the heath cudweed. Not in as much danger, but still rare, are wintergreen, serrated-leaved wintergreen and narrow buckler fern, all to be found in Perth & Kinross.

Ben Lawers is not only the highest peak and the highest of the Munros in Perth & Kinross, it is also a natural nature reserve. Its higher slopes provide perfect conditions for arctic and alpine species of plants that are otherwise rare in the UK. Sadly, climate change has been affecting these plants and there is concern that some may disappear altogether. In the meantime, there is still a wide variety of plant life to delight visitors, including the county's flower, the alpine or snow gentian. There are many other uncommon arctic and alpine species of plants around and on Ben Lawers, including a number of Britain's rarer sedges and ferns. At the right times of year, harebells, yarrow, tormentil and many other familiar flowers can be seen on the lower slopes. The mountain also supports all sorts of wildlife, from red deer to black grouse.

In addition to conserving flora and fauna on Ben Lawers, it is seen as vital to try to prevent further erosion of the mountain's peat by sheep, deer and wind erosion. By conserving it well, the peat will be able to contribute towards storing carbon dioxide more effectively. It is anticipated that with good management, the peat on Ben Lawers will be able to store as much carbon dioxide as two diesel cars would pump into the atmosphere annually. Different techniques are being tried and the project is ongoing at the time of writing.

While you are eating your fish supper at one of Loch Leven's nearby restaurants, your conversation might, if you are visiting in the summer, be about seeing ospreys swooping across the water to catch theirs earlier in the day. You can watch the loch's myriad bird-life from the RSPB's hides at the waterside, or through the spotting scopes provided free of charge in the cafeteria above their shop. Either way, you can be sure of seeing something interesting very quickly, as there are more freshwater breeding ducks here than anywhere else in inland Europe. It is also used as a staging post for thousands of migratory wildfowl, and pink footed geese arrive from Iceland in their tens of thousands during the autumn months. More common residents and visitors are lapwings, ringed plovers, swallows, curlews, kestrels, various thrushes and woodpeckers, as well as the various ubiquitous tit families, sparrow varieties and... well, the list could go on and on.

There are also wet grasslands, raised bog, willow and reed beds and a rich variety of plant life to see. There is interesting wildlife under the water too, in the form of its world famous and unique brown trout, *salmo levenensis*. It is similar to a sea trout in appearance but is described by the angling fraternity as having a *"graceful form and sporting qualities"* which makes it *"easily distinguished from any trout caught elsewhere"* and as a bonus it has a lovely flavour. Because it happily interbreeds with other types of trout and therefore non-conformist offspring are produced, you have to come to Loch Leven to find the genuine article. It has been introduced to rivers and lakes all over the world, but even when there have been no other types of trout around, its character still changes once it leaves its native Kinross.

There are a number of smaller areas in the region dedicated to preserving rare and endangered plant life and habitats. These are termed 'Important Plant Areas' and there are a number of them in Perth & Kinross including Crieff Woods, the Dunkeld-Blairgowrie Lochs, Rannoch Moor IPA and Black Wood of Rannoch.

Add to that the many 'Sites of Special Scientific Interest', 'Special Areas of Conservation' and 'Specially Protected Areas' which exist in Perth & Kinross and it becomes clear why this is such a magnificent part of Scotland to visit or live.

CHAPTER EIGHTEEN

'O may 't ne'er be a living plague'

PLAGUE

T
HE LAST CASE OF PLAGUE to occur in Scotland was in 1900 in Glasgow, with the loss of 16 of the 36 people infected in the outbreak. The first time the epidemic arrived in historic Perthshire was 1512 when it hit the city of Perth. It returned there several times after that, despite the fact that measures to prevent it arriving in the country at all had been put in place decades before similar precautions were taken in England. The Scots entirely blamed the English for the disease, being firmly of the belief that it was God's way of punishing those living south of the border for past transgressions.

The disease is believed to have been brought to Scotland by some of their own soldiers. On hearing that the plague had been killing off the citizens of Cumberland and Durham, the Scots massed their forces in the forest of Selkirk and waited for an opportune moment to invade. Before they could, they too were struck down and 5,000 of them died. Those who remained tried to get home. Many died on the way, but it is thought that those who did manage to get home introduced the disease into Scotland. There is a theory that it may have also arrived through Scotland's East Coast ports.

In the sixteenth and early seventeenth centuries, epidemics put a huge strain on Perth's economy, especially after the almost year-long outbreak starting in September 1584, with the death of over 1,400 of its citizens; and then another 600 died in the 1606/07 flare-up. At one point, there were only 370 inhabited houses left in Perth. Each outbreak of plague resulted in a loss of between 10 per cent and 20 per cent of the city's adult householders.

In a letter sent in 1512 to *"our lovitts the Provest, Baillies, and counsal of our burgh of Perth"*, James IV expresses the hope that they will staunch *"this contagious playg of pestilence now raiging in maist pairt of our territorie".* No such luck unfortunately.

There was obviously a scattered population in what is now the Perth & Kinross area, so you might think that losses were not as great as they might have been. Plague still had a proportionately devastating effect there too. The little village of Fortingall seems to have lost all but one of its inhabitants, an old woman who was believed to have buried every one of her fellow villagers. Their mass grave site (formerly a Bronze Age tumulus) is marked by a stone in a field opposite the Fortingall Hotel.

Things were not much better in the parish of Methven, a few miles west of Perth. In one of the later epidemics – September 1645 – there were only six survivors from Westwood and Myreside. Even more remote was Finlarig, close to Killin, then in Perthshire. After yet another visitation by the plague, among other diseases, its then landowner was reduced to asking that he pay less tax and supply fewer men for military service, due to how badly his estates had been affected.

The Black Castle of Moulin in the Tummel Valley, near Pitlochry, was abandoned altogether in the early sixteenth century in an effort to avoid the rest of the area contracting the disease. Depending on which account you read, it was either set on fire or it was destroyed by cannon shots after the entire complement of soldiers garrisoned there died from the plague.

CHAPTER NINETEEN

'Perhaps it may turn out a sang'

Poetry

A 2.2-MILE WAY-MARKED PATH AT TROCHRY, near Dunkeld, takes you on a lovely walk through various types of country and on different surfaces: *"to be as sensitive as possible to the wild terrain it passes through"*. This however is a walk with a difference: this one takes you along the Corbenic Poetry Path. The path is on an estate owned by the Corbenic Camphill Community, which is part of the International Camphill Movement for social renewal through community living.

To get there: from the south follow the A9 North from Perth. Just past Dunkeld Railway Station (on the left of the A9) you will find an exit for the A822 signposted for Crieff. Follow the A822 for a few miles. The Corbenic Poetry Path car park is on the right after the hamlet of Trochry. The path itself is fully way-marked.

On the path, you will find extracts from poetry which has been written by a number of modern Scottish poets. To make things even more interesting, the extracts are presented in a wide variety of ways and at different heights. They are carved on stones and granite, etched in glass or burned in wood on part of a tree and even beehives. Some pieces are on stones partially sunk into the ground, others are atop waist-high posts.

All the path's poems (in full), accompanied by stunning photographs, are available through the path's website in a 55-page A4 format book: **https://www.corbenicpoetrypath.com.**

There have been a number of poems written in the past by local poets or from elsewhere, but about what is now Perth & Kinross. Robert Burns, although not from the area, wrote several.

Robert Burns travelled around Scotland quite a lot in his short life (he died at the age of just 37), including Highland Perthshire during a three-week trip in 1787. He and his friend William Nicol left Edinburgh on the 25th of August that year, first going to Linlithgow and Stirling before they moved on to Perthshire, calling in at Crieff, Dunkeld and Aberfeldy as well as Kenmore on the shores of Loch Tay. During the course of their travels, they met Niel Gow, the famous Perthshire fiddle player, whose music inspired Burns to write several songs based on Gow's melodies. Describing his trip in his journal, Burns said that the *"journey through the Highlands was perfectly inspiring; and I hope I have laid in a good stock of new poetical ideas"*.

Despite his humble beginnings, Burns's poetry was so well received that he made friends in high places. He was described by a contemporary in Edinburgh as getting along easily with those of a higher social station than himself. Conversational skills and magnetic personality helped Burns enormously, and he did not have the cloddish, country bumpkin manners that they might have expected from a person with his lowly farming background.

Burns was invited to stay with the 4th Duke of Atholl at Blair Castle in 1787 and described his stay as two of the happiest days of his life. It was recommended to him that he should visit Bruar Water and, although he found the falls quite beautiful, he was appalled at the lack of trees and shrubs along the way. So, through his poetry – *The Humble Petition of Bruar Water* – he suggested that the duke should do something about it. Eventually, the duke did, but rather than planting the native trees and bushes Burns had suggested, he planted 120,000 larch. It was a good job Burns did not live to see it.

The Humble Petition of Bruar Water

My lord, I know your noble ear
Woe ne'er assails in vain;
Embolden'd thus, I beg you'll hear
Your humble slave complain,
How saucy Phoebus' scorching beams,
In flaming summer-pride,
Dry-withering, waste my foamy streams,
And drink my crystal tide.

The lightly-jumping, glowrin' trouts,
That thro' my waters play,
If, in their random, wanton spouts,
They near the margin stray;
If, hapless chance! they linger lang,
I'm scorching up so shallow,
They're left the whitening stanes amang,
In gasping death to wallow.

Last day I grat wi' spite and teen,
As poet Burns came by.
That, to a bard, I should be seen
Wi' half my channel dry;
A panegyric rhyme, I ween,
Ev'n as I was, he shor'd me;
But had I in my glory been,
He, kneeling, wad ador'd me.

Here, foaming down the skelvy rocks,
In twisting strength I rin;
There, high my boiling torrent smokes,
Wild-roaring o'er a linn:
Enjoying each large spring and well,
As Nature gave them me,
I am, altho' I say't mysel',
Worth gaun a mile to see.

Would then my noble master please
To grant my highest wishes,
He'll shade my banks wi' tow'ring trees,
And bonie spreading bushes.
Delighted doubly then, my lord,
You'll wander on my banks,
And listen mony a grateful bird
Return you tuneful thanks.

The sober lav'rock, warbling wild,
Shall to the skies aspire;
The gowdspink, Music's gayest child,
Shall sweetly join the choir;
The blackbird strong, the lintwhite clear,
The mavis mild and mellow;
The robin pensive Autumn cheer,
In all her locks of yellow.

This, too, a covert shall ensure,
To shield them from the storm;
And coward maukin sleep secure,
Low in her grassy form:
Here shall the shepherd make his seat,
To weave his crown of flow'rs;
Or find a shelt'ring, safe retreat,
From prone-descending show'rs.

And here, by sweet, endearing stealth,
Shall meet the loving pair,
Despising worlds, with all their wealth,
As empty idle care;
The flow'rs shall vie in all their charms,

The hour of heav'n to grace;
And birks extend their fragrant arms
To screen the dear embrace.

Here haply too, at vernal dawn,
Some musing bard may stray,
And eye the smoking, dewy lawn,
And misty mountain grey;
Or, by the reaper's nightly beam,
Mild-chequering thro' the trees,
Rave to my darkly dashing stream,
Hoarse-swelling on the breeze.

Let lofty firs, and ashes cool,
My lowly banks o'erspread,
And view, deep-bending in the pool,
Their shadow's wat'ry bed:
Let fragrant birks, in woodbines drest,
My craggy cliffs adorn;
And, for the little songster's nest,
The close embow'ring thorn.

So may old Scotia's darling hope,
Your little angel band
Spring, like their fathers, up to prop
Their honour'd native land!
So may, thro' Albion's farthest ken,
To social-flowing glasses,
The grace be – "Athole's honest men,
"And Athole's bonie lasses!"

('Laverock' = lark, 'gowdspink' = goldfinch, 'intwhite' = linnet and 'mavis' = song thrush.)

Burns had a habit of writing his poems on anything he could get access to, including scratching them on to windows or even carving them on trees. He also wrote one in pencil over the chimney-piece in the parlour of the Kenmore Hotel, Taymouth, when he stayed there. The poem is still there, today protected by glass. And, the seat he sat on while he wrote the poem is held at Perth Museum & Art Gallery. It can be seen by appointment.

Verses Written with a Pencil over the Chimneypiece in the Parlour of the Inn at Kenmore, Taymouth

These northern scenes with weary feet I trace;
O'er many a winding dale and painful steep,
Th' abodes of covey'd grouse and timid sheep,

My savage journey, curious, I pursue,
Till fam'd Breadalbane opens to my view. -
The meeting cliffs each deep-sunk glen divides,
The woods wild scatter'd clothe their ample sides;
Th' outstretching lake, imbosomed 'mong the hills,
The eye with wonder and amazement fills;
The Tay meand'ring sweet in infant pride,
The palace rising on his verdant side,
The lawns wood-fring'd in Nature's native taste,
The hillocks dropt in Nature's careless haste,
The arches striding o'er the new-born stream,
The village glittering in the noontide beam-

Poetic ardours in my bosom swell,
Lone wand'ring by the hermit's mossy cell;
The sweeping theatre of hanging woods,
Th' incessant roar of headlong tumbling floods-
Here Poesy might wake her heav'n-taught lyre,
And look through Nature with creative fire;
Here, to the wrongs of Fate half reconcil'd,
Misfortunes lighten'd steps might wander wild;
And Disappointment, in these lonely bounds,
Find balm to soothe her bitter, rankling wounds:
Here heart-struck Grief might heav'nward stretch her

Burns was also impressed with the Birks of Aberfeldy (there is a statue to him there, seated on a bench) and the Falls of Moness. He wrote a poem about them in 1787.

The Birks of Aberfeldy

Will ye go, will ye go,
Bonie lassie, will ye go
To the birks of Aberfeldy!

Now Simmer blinks on flowery braes,
And o'er the crystal streamlets plays;
Come let us spend the lightsome days,
In the birks of Aberfeldy.
Bonie lassie, &c.

While o'er their heads the hazels hing,
The little birdies blythely sing,
Or lightly flit on wanton wing,
In the birks of Aberfeldy.
Bonie lassie, &c.

The braes ascend like lofty wa's,
The foaming stream deep-roaring fa's,
O'erhung wi' fragrant spreading shaws-
The birks of Aberfeldy.
Bonie lassie, &c.

The hoary cliffs are crown'd wi' flowers,
White o'er the linns the burnie pours,
And rising, weets wi' misty showers
The birks of Aberfeldy.
Bonie lassie, &c.

Let Fortune's gifts at randoe flee,
They ne'er shall draw a wish frae me;
Supremely blest wi' love and thee,
In the birks of Aberfeldy.
Bonie lassie, &c.

Chorus. – *Bonie lassie, will ye go*

('birk' = 'birch'.)
As an interesting aside – and many thousands of miles from Perth & Kinross – a crater on Mercury is named after Burns.

Then there is the poet from Kinross-shire who inspired him,

Michael Bruce – also known as the 'Poet of Loch Leven'. Sadly, Bruce died aged only 21, but his fine pastoral poetry was an inspiration to Burns as well as other poets. He knew he was dying from consumption and wrote about it in *To the Cuckoo* – even though it was unacceptable to mention your own impending demise in those days!

To the Cuckoo

Hail! beauteous Stranger of the wood!
Attendant on the Spring!
Now heav'n repairs thy rural seat,
And woods thy welcome sing.

Soon as the daisy decks the green,
Thy certain voice we hear:
Hast thou a star to guide thy path,
Or mark the rolling year?

Delightful visitant! with thee
I hail the time of flow'rs,
When heav'n is fill'd with music sweet
Of birds among the bow'rs.

The schoolboy wand'ring in the wood
To pull the flow'rs so gay,
Starts, thy curious voice to hear,
And imitates thy lay.

Soon as the pea puts on the bloom,
Thou fly'st thy vocal vale,
An annual guest, in other lands,
Another Spring to hail.

Sweet bird! thy bow'r is ever green,
Thy sky is ever clear;
Thou hast no sorrow in thy song,
No winter in thy year!

Alas! sweet bird! not so my fate,
Dark scowling skies I see
Fast gathering round, and fraught with woe
And wintry years to me.

O could I fly, I'd fly with thee:
We'd make, with social wing,
Our annual visit o'er the globe,
Companions of the Spring.

William McGonagall is mentioned in the section on *The Fair Maid of Perth*. I only subjected you to three verses of his poetry. Here is one he wrote about Loch Leven. As usual, McGonagall's information is inaccurate. He mentions *"Benarty's rugged hills"*, but Benarty is just one hill in the Cleish Hills range, the highest being Dumglow. At least he got the direction of the two ranges he mentioned right, but he failed to mention the Ochil Hills to the north and the loch is not 'very deep' as lochs go.

Loch Leven

Beautiful Loch Leven, near by Kinross
For a good day's fishing the angler is seldom at a loss,
For the Loch it abounds with pike and trout,
Which can be had for the catching without any doubt;
And the scenery around it is most beautiful to be seen,
Especially the Castle, wherein was imprisoned Scotland's
ill-starred Queen.

Then there's the lofty Lomond Hills on the Eastern side,
And the loch is long, very deep, and wide;
Then on the Southern side there's Benarty's rugged hills,
And from the tops can be seen the village of Kinross with
its spinning mills.

The big house of Kinross is very handsome to be seen,
With its beautiful grounds around it, and the lime trees so green
And 'tis a magnificent sight to see, on a fine summer afternoon,
The bees extracting honey from the leaves when in full bloom.

There the tourist can enjoy himself and while away the hours,
Underneath the lime trees shady bowers,
And listen to the humming of the busy bees,
While they are busy gathering honey from the lime trees.

Then there's the old burying ground near by Kinross,
And the dead that lie there turned into dusty dross,
And the gravestones are all in a state of decay,
And the old wall around it is mouldering away.

William Soutar appears in the section on famous people; it is nonetheless fitting that two of his poems also feature in this chapter.

Cradle Sang

Fa' owre, fa' owre, my hinny,
There's monie a weary airt;
And nae end to the traikin,
For man has a hungry hert.
What wud ye hae for ferlie
And no ken the want o' mair?
The sün for a gowdan aipple:
The müne for a siller pear.

Yon Toun

1

Hae ye come in be yon toun
Ablow the craigie knowes?
Hae ye come in be yon toun
Whaur the clear water rows?

*

2

Birk and rodden on the brae,
Hawthorn in the hauch;
And clear water churlin by
The elder and the sauch

3

At day–daw and at grey–fa'
The merry bells ding doun:
At day-daw and grey-fa'
There's music in yon toun

4

Merlie and mavie whistle clear;
And when the hour is still
Haikers owre the auld brig hear
The gowk upon the hill.

5

Wha wudna bide in yon toun
Ablow the craigie knowes?
Wha wudna bide in yon toun
Whaur the clear water rows?

Perthshire poet William Renton painted a lovely word picture in his late nineteenth-century poem *Mountain Twilight.*

Mountain Twilight

The hills slipped over each on each
Till all their changing shadows died.
Now in the open skyward reach
The lights grow solemn side by side.
While of these hills the westermost
Rears high his majesty of coast
In shifting waste of dim-blue brine
And fading olive hyaline;
Till all the distance overflows,
The green in watchet and the blue
In purple. Now they fuse and close -
A darkling violet, fringed anew
With light that on the mountains soar,
A dusky flame on tranquil shores;
Kindling the summits as they grow
In audience to the skies that call,
Ineffable in rest and all
The pathos of the afterglow.

* * *

John Davidson was not from Perth & Kinross though taught at Perth Academy (1878–81) and wrote about Perthshire and Kinross-shire. This is an extract from his poem *Winter in Strathearn*.

Winter in Strathearn

The twinkling Earn, like a blade in the snow,
The low hills scalloped against the high,
The high hills leaping upon the low,
And the amber wine in the cup of the sky,
With the white world creaming over the rim,
She watched; and a keen aroma rose,
Embodied, a star above the snows;
For when the west sky-edge grows dim,
When lights are silver and shades are brown,
Behind Torlum the sun goes down;
And from Glenartney, night by night;
The full fair star of evening creeps;
Though spectral branches clasp it tight,
Like magic from their hold it leaps.
And reaches heaven at once. Her sight
Gathers the star, and in her eyes
She meekly wears heaven's fairest prize.

He also wrote of Kinnoull Hill.

Kinnoull Hill

We sat on the verge of the steep
In a coign where the east wind failed.
In heaven's top, cradled, asleep,
The young sun basked, and deep
Into space the universe sailed.
And eastward the cliff rose higher,
And westward it sloped to the town,
That smoked like a smouldering fire
Built close about spire after spire;
And the smoke was pale-blue and brown.

The smell of the turf and the pine
Wound home to our heart's warm core;
And we knew by a secret sign
That earth is your mother and mine;
And we loved each other the more.

And out of the rock, scarred and bare,
The daws came crying in crowds,
And tossed themselves into the air,
And flew up and down, here and there.
And cast flying shadows, like clouds.

We heard not the lark, but we heard
The mellow, ineffable tune
Of a sweet-piping, wood-haunting bird.
Our heart-strings were stricken and stirred,
And we two were happy that noon.

CHAPTER TWENTY

'I wander in the ways of men'

RAILWAYS

THE EARLIEST SCOTTISH RAILWAY to be incorporated by private Act of Parliament was the Kilmarnock & Troon (in Ayrshire) in 1808. It was 40 years later before the railway arrived in Perthshire, and it was 1855 before an Act of Parliament authorised the building of a 14-mile branch line from Ladybank in Fife to Kinross. Construction began early in 1856 and an application was made to Parliament later that year to extend it to nearby Milnathort.

LIFE WOULD HAVE BEEN A LOT EASIER for the Fife & Kinross Railway Company (FKRC) had the Edinburgh, Perth & Dundee Railway Company been prepared to run their trains along the line, but they were not. So, for a brief time it looked as if the company would have a railway line, but no trains travelling along it. In spite of this, the FKRC managed to acquire a couple of locomotives of their own, which were promptly named Loch Leven Castle and Falkland Castle. There were eventually three railway companies operating in the second smallest shire in Scotland: Fife & Kinross Railway, Kinross-shire Railway and Devon Valley Railway.

Sir William Tite designed many of the early railway stations in Britain, including Perth Railway Station, which was started in 1848 and completed in 1850. It began life as a station for the Highland, Caledonian and North British Railways. Originally known as Perth General Railway Station, its name was changed simply to Perth Station in 1952. This large through station originally had six platforms. It now has seven, five of which are for through trains.

Sometimes it was felt that a short stretch of line did not warrant the use of a locomotive, but passengers still needed to be carried along it. This was when the steam railcar came into its own. James Samuel, a locomotive engineer with the Eastern Counties Railway, designed the first steam railcar (very occasionally referred to as a rail bus). This was a small passenger coach with the locomotive as an integral part of it, rather than as a separate vehicle hauling carriages behind it.

An experimental unit was built by William Bridges Adams in 1847. It was 12 feet 6 inches long. When Samuel and Adams built the Fairfield steam carriage the next year, it was two-and-a-half times larger than its predecessor. Although both the third-class and the boiler sections were open to the elements, the second-class section was covered. Many of these steam railcars bore a passing resemblance to railway carriages we could recognise today. However, a few were designed so that the covered areas looked more like the horse-drawn carriages passengers would have been familiar with.

Some of Perth & Kinross's railway past is not even visible above ground, examples of which are the two Glenfarg railway tunnels which pass deep beneath the Ochil hills.

The line itself was interesting in that different parts of it were built and owned by different companies at one time. Sadly, the line was one of Dr Beeching's casualties, being closed down on the

15th of June 1964. These days, it makes for a walk with a difference. The tunnels are both a third of a mile long, but if you plan on walking through them (which you can) make sure you take a torch with you. Halfway along there is a bend, after which you will find yourself in pitch darkness and you will definitely need your torch.

To get there, Fife Walking gives the following directions:

The walk can be started from the Bein Inn Hotel at the junction of the A912/B996 or from laybys on route. If parking at the hotel, please ask permission as their car park is for customer use. From the hotel walk north along the A912 for about 200m to a farm track on your left opposite a road signed for 'Binn Eco Park' (a landfill site). This section of the road can be busy and there is no pavement so take extreme care. (If the sun isn't out or you don't have a compass with you, head in the direction of Bridge of Earn).

CHAPTER TWENTY-ONE

'Flow gently, I'll sing thee a song in thy praise'

Rivers, Lochs and Waterfalls

Water makes a significant contribution to the charm and beauty of Perth & Kinross. The picturesque nature of its rivers, lochs and waterfalls even inspired Robert Burns to write several poems, including one about Loch Tay, which begins:

Th' outstretching lake, imbosomed 'mong the hills,
The eye with wonder and amazement fills

Rivers

THERE ARE ABOUT EIGHTEEN RIVERS IN PERTHSHIRE, four in Kinross-shire – the Leven, Garney and the North and South Queich – and innumerable burns in both counties. Of these, the river that carries the greatest volume of water in the whole of the British Isles is the River Tay, even though it is only the seventh longest river in the UK. It carries as much water along its course as the Thames and Severn put together, at 100 cubic metres per second by water volume discharged into the sea. In his paper 'Rising from the Waves:

The Development of the Historic Burgh of Perth', David Bowler describes this fact in a very dramatic light: *"When the snows melt, enormous flows can be released, up to seven million tonnes per hour"*.

The Tay may not be the longest river in the UK, but it is, nonetheless, the longest river in Scotland, its length varying from 117 to 123 miles depending on which reference you are reading. It is agreed, nonetheless, that the Tay's source is a spring on Ben Lui (Beinn Laoigh) in Argyll and that it then flows east, becoming tidal for its last 20 miles or so at Perth. The river is not called the Tay for the whole of its length, it only becomes the Tay once it has passed through its namesake loch, but it is the same river that bubbled out of that mountain spring.

Four lochs are fed by the Tay on its way to the sea: Lochs Rannoch, Ericht, Earn and Bà. The river has numerous tributaries of varying sizes, the most important of these are the rivers Lyon, Tummel, Isla, Almond, Earn and Braan.

This is a river with a long history of flooding the city of Perth. There were 34 floods recorded between the thirteenth century and the twentieth century. As mentioned elsewhere in this book, in the thirteenth century the Tay flooded to such an extent that it swept away the bridge, the castle and jolly nearly took William I (the Lion) with it.

The bridge disappeared again in 1648, and in 1774 rapid snowmelt, combined with a build-up of ice, jammed under the bridge, dammed the river and caused further severe flooding. This not only inundated the town, but also caused damage to ships docked in the quay, which at that time was much nearer the bridge than the harbour is today. A similar blockage in 1814 caused such bad flooding that ships were washed ashore! Not surprising when you consider the river was 23 feet 'Above Ordnance Datum (AOD)' (the height relative to the mean sea level at Newlyn, Cornwall). It was nearly as bad in 1990, reaching 19 feet, but Perth's flood defences built 20 years earlier held – just about. It was decided that the city needed better protection than it had, but before plans could be implemented, the Tay struck again in 1993. This time it flooded to a height of 21 feet AOD, covering the centre of Perth and both the Inches.

It is interesting to note that the word 'Inch' derives from the Gaelic 'innis' and means, among other things, *"a low-lying tract of ground on a river bank (sometimes cut off at high tide)"*. From the sound of it, the Inches have a very long history of being flooded by the waters of their neighbouring river.

Lochs

ALTHOUGH THERE ARE ANY NUMBER of very small lochs scattered about in the region, I have chosen to mention 13 of the bigger ones, three of which are shared with other Scottish council areas.

Loch Ericht is partially in Perth & Kinross, the rest of it is in the Highland Council area. Loch Earn is shared with Stirling Council, as is one of the deepest lochs in Scotland, Loch Tay. Loch Freuchie and a group of smaller lochs – Loch of Clunie, Marlee Loch, Loch of Craiglush, Loch of the Lowes and Butterstone Loch – lie west of Blairgowrie and Dunkeld, forming a chain of five 'kettle hole lochs' which is deemed a 'Special Area of Conservation'. ('Kettle hole' lochs and lakes are formed in depressions left in the ground after buried blocks of glacier ice have melted.) Loch Tummel lies west of Pitlochry and Loch Rannoch, west of that again. Then there is Loch Faskally, which is actually a man-made reservoir.

There are two bodies of water called Loch Leven in Scotland, a sea loch south of Fort William and the largest freshwater loch in the Lowlands at Kinross. Nestling among three ranges of hills, the Ochil,

Lomond and Cleish Hills, the Kinross loch used to hold more water than it does now. Things changed dramatically when, between 1828 and 1832, to enable the Laird of Kinross to expand the territory he owned by reclaiming all his land covered by water, the bed of the River Leven was lowered, the river course straightened, and sluice-gates installed. Effectively the loch shrank by a quarter of its original size. The idea originated with Thomas Graham in the late eighteenth century and was carried out by his trustees after his death. So, where water once lapped close to the walls of the castle where Mary, Queen of Scots, was kept prisoner, 300 years later, following a 4 feet 6 inches drop in the water level, the island expanded to the 8 acres it is today. The island had always been significant: there was a fort on it even before the rule of the area's seventh/eighth-century Pictish king Brude. Parts of the present castle date from the thirteenth century.

There is plenty to do and see around Loch Leven, from quietly sitting and watching the abundant bird-life, to circumnavigating the loch's heritage trail by foot, on two wheels or by wheelchair/electric scooter. You can do the trail in five short stages or join them together for longer stretches to suit your own inclination, followed by something to eat and drink at one of several eateries overlooking the loch.

Waterfalls

ROBERT BURNS WAS SO IMPRESSED with the Birks of Aberfeldy and the Falls of Moness, which he saw there, that he wrote a poem to them in 1787, *The Birks of Aberfeldy*, which features in the section on poetry.

There are many other lovely waterfalls in Perth & Kinross that Burns could have found equally impressive. The 700 feet high Allt da Ghob waterfall in Glen Lyon is but one example. In his book *The Gaelic Topography of Scotland, and What It Proves, Explained,* James Alexander Robertson translates Allt da Ghob thus: *"there is a stream with a very singular name: it is called the 'Alltandaghob' … meaning 'the stream of the two beaks' and arises from two streams coming from two points of land and then joining"*.

In addition, there is the Allt Mor Waterfall at the eastern end of Loch Rannoch, the Falls of Acharn south-west of Aberfeldy, the Black Spout waterfall, near Pitlochry, and the Deil's Cauldron, near Comrie. If you do not like to stray too far from a bit of shopping, then the Falls of Bruar is the place to go.

A great place to view the Black Linn Falls, which is in the National Trust for Scotland's Hermitage woodland at Dunkeld, is from a folly built for that very purpose. Ossian's Hall, built in 1757 as a memorial to the third century bard of that name, looks fairly unprepossessing from the outside. In its day, the inside was a different matter altogether. An inner hall had mirrors covering its walls and ceiling reflecting images of the waterfall from all directions. Stained-glass windows were coloured red and green, the coloured light filtering through on to the mirrors and adding to the strange illusion of having coloured water coming at you from every angle.

Following vandalisation of Ossian's Hall in 1869, instead of carrying out repair work, the place was left to decay. Then in 1944, the Duke of Atholl's widow gifted it and the coniferous woodland alongside the River Braan to the National Trust for Scotland, who commissioned Sir Basil Spence to renovate it. Ossian's Hall is no longer a hall of mirrors and stained-glass windows, but the scene from the viewing platform above the waterfall remains spectacular.

CHAPTER TWENTY-TWO

'For thus the Royal mandate ran'

ROYALS

Perth & Kinross has played host to a wide variety of royals, most of them willing visitors but one who certainly was not. Many of those who tarried within the area's borders were home grown – but not all of them; and one Perthshire lass gained her royal status only after leaving Scotland's shores altogether.

CHARLES I AND BONNIE PRINCE CHARLIE

IN 1663, CHARLES I *"sat upon the wall next to the water of Tay"* to watch members of the Glovers Incorporation *"perform on a floating stage of timber"*. The performance he watched was a sword dance. Charles was in Scotland to attend his coronation, which took place eight years after he had been crowned in Westminster Abbey in London. The king wanted Scottish bishops to be appointed by the Crown, the same as in England; he also believed that the king ruled by divine right. His Scottish Presbyterian subjects disagreed with both notions. This led to the formation of the Covenanters, who believed that Christ was the head of the Church, not the king.

Bonnie Prince Charlie, or to give him his full name Charles Edward Louis John Casimir Sylvester Severino Maria Stuart, was born in Rome in 1720 and died there in 1788. Charles Stuart firmly believed that his father should sit on the throne of Great Britain, not George II. He returned to Scotland in 1745, landing near Glenfinnan, on the west coast of Scotland, and planned to march to London to claim what he

saw as his family's rightful inheritance. The small following with whom he started out gradually grew as he went on a fundraising tour through Scotland. This brought Charles Stuart to Perth, where he held a planning meeting in Room 20 of the Salutation Hotel. Allegedly, Charles Stuart demanded that Perth should give him a donation of £500, but I have been unable to establish whether his demand was met or, indeed, if he even made it.

Charles Stuart is also supposed to have a connection with the Drummond Hotel in Crieff, where he held his last council of war.

DULEEP SINGH

A TRUE ROYAL IN EVERY SENSE OF THE WORD was the last Maharaja of the Sikh Empire, Duleep Singh. After spending time living in Scotland he became affectionately known as 'The Black Prince of Perthshire'.

Following a period of chaos in his own country of Punjab, Singh became Maharaja when he was only seven years old, with the throne changing hands four times in as many years before Duleep Singh succeeded to it. Singh's country was then annexed by the British East India Company, who deposed him when he was 11. The boy's mother, who had acted as regent, was jailed and Singh was sent to live with a Christian family some distance from his native Punjab. Under that family's influence, Singh became a Christian himself. He went to Britain in 1854 and, being a royal in his own right, Queen Victoria was happy to receive him at court. In fact, he was a frequent guest at Buckingham Palace and often stayed there.

Singh moved to Scotland in 1855 while still in his early teens, but as a ward of Sir John and Lady Login. Castle Menzies, near Aberfeldy, was leased for him and when that lease expired, he rented a mansion in the tiny hamlet of Auchlyne (in Perthshire at that time), near Stirling, from the Earl of Breadalbane. Singh not only lived a life of luxury, he also liked wearing a kilt. One of the pastimes he enjoyed was hawking and he was a founder member of the Old Hawking Society, which was later re-established as The British Falconers' Club. After that, he moved to the Grandtully Estate, north of Aberfeldy, staying for a while, before returning to India to rescue his mother. Singh brought her back to London where she lived for a few years until her death. When Singh took her body back to India to be cremated he met the woman who later became his wife and the pair returned to Scotland where their first child was born.

Sadly, the baby died when he was only 24 hours old; he is buried in the little graveyard at Kenmore, a small village at the northern end of Loch Tay.

Accounts of the Maharaja's life say he presented the magnificent 105-carat Koh-I-Noor diamond to Queen Victoria as a gift and there is at least one photograph showing that she wore it in a brooch. It is now set in the late Queen Mother's crown. While it is true that Singh gave it to Queen Victoria, he was just ten years old at the time! What most accounts fail to point out is that he was made to hand it over by the British East India Company under the terms of the Treaty of Lahore, which had been amended so that Singh was required not only to give away the diamond, but also his claim to sovereignty.

Singh moved from Scotland to the south of England and later in his life returned to his Sikh faith. He died in Paris aged 55.

* * *

EMPRESS EUGÉNIE

EMPRESS EUGÉNIE OF FRANCE, wife of Napoleon III, visited Scotland in 1860, and among other places visited Blair Castle. Eugénie was a Spanish countess whose mother was of Scottish and Belgian parentage. In 1853, she married Napoleon III, who came from common Corsican stock a mere couple of generations earlier. No wonder her side of the family considered that she had married beneath her!

HELEN GLOAG

THE MOST UNLIKELY ROYAL to be associated with Perth & Kinross was a blacksmith's daughter, Helen Gloag, born in January 1750 in Wester Pett, a hamlet near Muthill, about 20 miles west of Perth. Gloag's mother died when she was young, and her father remarried. She did not get on at all with her step-mother and at 19 decided to join the many Scots who were emigrating to America at that time. She may have been going to the Carolinas, which was a popular destination for people from Scotland (in most cases driven by poverty, rather than family upsets). A couple of weeks into the 50-day journey her ship was captured in the North Atlantic by Barbary pirates, who regularly operated in the area. Although the men on board were all killed, the women were seen as financial assets and were sold into slavery.

Helen's long red hair, green eyes and pale skin made her a particularly striking looking young woman and it was her looks that were her deliverance at the slave market and later. She was spotted by a wealthy Moroccan, who bought her and gave her as a gift to the Sultan of Morocco. Instead of using her as a slave, he added her to his harem. Gloag gradually worked her way up the social scale, finally becoming his principal wife with the title Empress of Morocco. She took full advantage of her elevated position and is credited with reducing the activities of the pirates and securing the release of some captured seafarers and slaves. Gloag was able to write letters home and was even allowed to have her brother come to stay with her.

Her fate is uncertain. The sultan died in 1790 and his throne was seized by one of his sons, who eliminated any potential rivals by killing them off. Sadly, this included Helen's two sons, though it is not known whether Helen suffered the same fate.

JAMES I

AFTER ATTENDING A GENERAL COUNCIL held in Perth early in February 1437, James I and his wife went back to their lodgings at the Blackfriars Monastery where they stayed for several weeks more. Looking back at events from this distance in history, the king seemed blissfully unaware of just how much he had angered his nobles, one way and another.

For one thing, James had replaced the Bishop of Dunkeld Cathedral's chapter (the bishop's advisers) with his nephew. That came on top of increasing taxation several times, the money gathered in being used, among other things, towards paying off his £40,000 ransom debt owed to the English. Added to that, James attacked those of his own nobles whom he perceived as enemies in order to bolster his personal authority, starting with executing the Duke of Albany and his sons. James ignored Scottish hostages in England who had been exchanged to help secure his own release, keeping their ransom money to pay for frivolous improvements to his various homes. To add insult to injury, the king's siege of the English-held Roxburgh Castle had failed miserably, and he wanted even more taxes levied to pay for having another go.

James might have suspected something was not right when Sir Robert Graham, the speaker of the General Council, denounced and then attempted to arrest his monarch at a meeting of the General Council the previous year. Instead Sir Robert found himself imprisoned in Dunbar Castle, although he managed to escape a few months later.

Enough was enough, and so, led by an understandably disgruntled Sir Robert Graham, accompanied by the Earl of Atholl plus about 30 other men (including the king's uncle), the group set off for Blackfriars Monastery on the evening of 20 February 1437.

The king and queen were relaxing in their rooms with very few of their servants in attendance. The king's chamberlain (who managed the household) happened to be the Earl of Atholl's grandson and heir. He made sure that the conspirators could easily access the royal apartments by removing the bolt on their chamber's door. The chamberlain reckoned without the bravery of Catherine Douglas, the queen's lady-in-waiting. She used her arm as a replacement for the missing bolt, thus giving the royal couple a bit of extra time to try and escape. In the event, although her mistress managed to survive, the king did not. Some 400 years after the king's murder, Dante Gabriel Rossetti's 1881 poem *The King's Tragedy* recorded in poetic form the bravery of the young woman who was to become known to history as Kate Barlass.

According to the fifteenth-century *Scotichronicon*, written by Walter Bower, a contemporary of James I, the king was excellent at sport, and one of the sports he thoroughly enjoyed was tennis. When in Perth, he played on a paved area just behind his apartments at the monastery, but he got fed up with losing tennis balls down an outlet drain which also served the royal chambers. So, earlier in the month, he had ordered the outlet to be bricked up. Problem solved. As it turned out, this was not such a good idea after all.

When he finally cottoned on that his life was in danger James thought he could escape by tearing up the floorboards, ducking into the waste pipe that ran beneath them and led to the drain at the tennis court, then make his way out from there. The bricked-up outlet prevented him doing that, nor could he escape from the room, which was now filled with his murderous enemies. And so, James I was stabbed to death.

JAMES IV AND MARGARET TUDOR

SIX MILES WEST OF PERTH LIES METHVEN CASTLE. During the last decade of the fifteenth century James IV visited it several times. His wife however had a much closer connection to the place: she died there (due to a stroke, it is thought) on the 18th of October 1541. She was 52.

As a way of sealing the peace between Scotland and England, Henry VII's oldest daughter, the 13-year-old Margaret Tudor, was married to the Scottish king, James IV (aged 30). This was done by proxy while she was still in London. Margaret Tudor then travelled up to Scotland where the marriage was confirmed in person at Holyrood Abbey on the 8th of August 1503. Both royals were destined to have connections with Perthshire, Margaret Tudor more so than her husband.

Their 10-year-long marriage ended when James was killed at the Battle of Flodden in 1513. He was the last British monarch to be killed in battle. A year later, Margaret Tudor secretly married Archibald Douglas, the 6th Earl of Angus in Kinnoull Parish Church (about half a mile east of the centre of Perth). Little did she know that he not only had a lover tucked quietly away, he intended to keep her in tow and used his wife's money to do so. No wonder Margaret Tudor asked Pope Clement VI for a divorce from her adulterous husband. This was granted in March 1527.

Her next and final marriage was to Henry Stewart, 1st Lord Methven. The marriage took place in December 1527 and this husband turned out to be as unfaithful as her previous one – and just as free with her money. Margaret Tudor came to terms with all this – she had to because the Pope refused to sanction another divorce. In any case, her son, James V, was absolutely against it. And so, Margaret Tudor found herself living at Methven Castle; and dying there. (Her great grandson was to become the king who united the thrones of England and Scotland.)

JAMES V

JAMES V WATCHED *Ane Satyre of the thrie Estaitis* performed in 1535 in an amphitheatre outside Perth's city walls, somewhere in the area where the St Catherine's Retail Park is today.

MACBETH

THANKS TO SHAKESPEARE, Macbeth is most often associated with Birnam and its elderly oak tree in the wood there. Notably, he also had a connection with Loch Leven in Kinross-shire.

It was normal practice in medieval times for royalty to keep on very good terms with the Church. It was believed that by donating substantial gifts, in a wide variety of forms, you would be smoothing your way to Heaven. Macbeth, together with his wife Gruoch, achieved this in part by granting some land to the Culdee community at a place which is now known as Kirkness at the south-eastern end of Lochleven. The Culdees was a monastic society whose members led a hermit-like lifestyle and whose order originated in Ireland.

Macbeth was so far removed from the evil character portrayed by

Shakespeare that he even travelled the 1,243 miles on pilgrimage to Rome (*c.*1050) where he was reported to have *"scattered silver like seed to the poor"*. This might sound like a long and arduous journey, and no doubt it was, but Macbeth was not alone in making it. Although Macbeth was the only Scottish king to make the pilgrimage to Rome, it was not an uncommon journey for monks and royals to make at the time; King Cnut also made the same journey.

MARY, QUEEN OF SCOTS

ANOTHER MUCH LESS WILLING VISITOR to Loch Leven was the pregnant 25-year-old Mary, Queen of Scots, in mid-June 1567. After a four-hour forced ride through the night from Edinburgh, when she finally reached the castle in the middle of the loch, the queen was not at all well. For more than a fortnight she was so poorly her captors were unsure if she would live or die.

Her equerry, Sir Robert Melville, visited the queen repeatedly in an effort to persuade her to abdicate in favour of her infant son. She kept refusing, fearful that if she abdicated then the next step would be for her baby son, the future James VI, to be murdered and the throne seized by her enemies. The ride and stress, combined with her desperate situation, led, in all likelihood, to her having a miscarriage in July. It is believed that she was three months pregnant and that she miscarried twins, who were buried at the castle. There is, however, another version of the story which says that Mary gave birth to a daughter at full term. The tale goes on to say that the baby was smuggled out of the castle and taken to France, where she was sent to a convent at Soissons. She then grew up to become a nun.

Shortly after her miscarriage, when Mary was very ill and weak, Sir Robert Melville called on her yet again to try to persuade her to abdicate. This time, Lord Lindsay and Lord Ruthven were waiting outside the door of her room. When she still refused to sign the abdication papers they lost patience. They marched in and ordered her two maids to leave. Lord Lindsay then threatened to cut her throat if she did not sign. And so, the terrified young woman abdicated in favour of her baby son.

Mary made two attempts to escape. The first failed when the boatman who was to row her across the loch realised that the lovely smooth white hands he had spotted could not belong to the 'washerwoman' he was supposed to be taking home after work. And consequently, she was returned to her prison tower.

With the help of Willie and George Douglas (two of her captor's sons no less) Mary's second attempt was successful. This escape has all the elements that would be more at home in a Hollywood film. The two lads had concocted all sorts of escape plans for the queen, most of them not really feasible. They had helped her with her first attempt too and when their father got to hear about it he sent the older one, George, back to the mainland and banned him from ever returning to the island. Unperturbed, George found a way to get back by pretending he was going to France and asking to come back to the island one last time to bid everyone goodbye. One of George's sisters persuaded her father to let George do that. The stage was set.

The only way out of the castle was by the postern gate, which was locked at 7.00pm each night, after which the key was handed to Sir William Douglas and the guards went off duty. The problem was that Sir William kept the key beside him at all times. So young Willie threw a party, during which he managed to replace the keys beside his father with a false set. Locking the postern gate behind them, the little group of fugitives consisting of Mary, one of her maids and the two Douglas boys made for the boats. Some accounts say that Willie dropped the keys into the loch and they were only found in 1805. Mary's own version says he dropped them into the mouth of a cannon outside the castle.

Waiting for them on the shore were a group of Mary's friends who had been secretly summoned from Edinburgh. Of course, everyone inside the castle stayed inside the castle – they had no choice as they were locked in.

QUEEN VICTORIA

QUEEN VICTORIA AND PRINCE ALBERT visited Scotland many times, staying in Perthshire on a number of occasions. Their first visit was in September 1842, when they stayed at Scone Palace on their way for a three-day visit to Taymouth Castle, where their host was Lord Breadalbane. On the way there, they were treated to a sumptuous lunch in Dunkeld, as guests of the Duke of Atholl.

A Mrs Maule, wife of the Liberal MP for Perthshire at the time, was also a guest at the castle and kept a diary of events which makes interesting reading. Among other things, she records that 730 people were catered for each day, of whom 300 were fed in the castle and the rest in nearby locations. As well as consuming copious amounts of beef, mutton, lamb, venison and game birds between them, the guests also downed 160 gallons of whisky and 900 gallons of ale and beer each day.

On another trip in 1844, the royal family and their entourage took over Blair Castle and stayed for three weeks. The queen was guarded by a group of men in the Duke of Atholl's employ and in return for that she awarded them the Queen's Colours. In effect, this meant the duke now had a private army and still does. Known these days as the Atholl Highlanders, it is the only private army in Europe.

The George Inn, now the Royal George Hotel, had a surprise royal visit in September 1848 and only half-an-hours' notice to prepare, when Queen Victoria and Prince Albert with their children unexpectedly stayed overnight. Normally they returned to London by sea from Balmoral, but on this occasion the sea was far too rough, so they travelled by train and decided to stay overnight in Perth to break the long journey. The Royal Warrant, enabling the hotel to change its name from The George Inn to The Royal George Hotel, still hangs in the hotel's lounge.

The Duchess of Argyll was a close friend of the queen, so Victoria stopped at Blair Castle to visit the seriously ill Duke in 1863. He died early in the following year.

During another stay at Balmoral in 1865 Victoria made time to call on her friend again, who was by now living in Dunkeld; she stayed for a few days on this occasion. The following year, Victoria paid another visit to the Dowager Duchess; this was to be the queen's penultimate visit to Perthshire.

When Queen Victoria visited Loch Tummel, Pitlochry in 1866, she was under the impression that 'Queen's View' had been thus named in honour of her visit. However, it might just as easily have been named after Queen Isabella, first wife of Robert the Bruce, who in the fourteenth century also stopped there in the course of her travels.

CHAPTER TWENTY-THREE

His ancient, trusty, drouthy crony'

STANDING STONES

There are more than 100 stone circles in Perthshire, or the remains of them, and two sites with standing stones in Kinross-shire.

ALTHOUGH standing stones are often referred to as 'Roman Stones', in fact, they predate the Romans by 2,000-3,000 years. Their purpose is unknown, but there are a number of theories. These include alignment with sunrise, alignment with sunsets or alignments with the stars. Other thoughts suggest that they were burial grounds, had religious significance or were simply meeting places. The claim that they may have been burial grounds is supported by the fact that cremated ashes have been found close to and among some standing stones.

For instance, in Kinross-shire, there is a pair of stones standing in a field at Orwell by the A911. They are made of whinstone (quartz dolerite) and can be easily seen from the road. The western stone had fallen over at some point and it was re-erected; then both stones were embedded in cement to stop them falling over again. Prior to this being done, several cremation deposits were found; it is thought that these were placed at the time of the erection of the stones, which points to burials and the stones being associated. There is another pair of stones at Dundonnachie, near Kinross, which are described by archae-ologists as having characteristics *"similar to other 'Perthshire pairs'* [so] *there is a possibility they may fall into this category"*.

As is so often the case, stories and legends associated with standing stones abound. As well as those connected with fairies, mentioned in another part of this book, there are several stones known as 'Witches Stones'. These can be found at Meikle Obney, near Dunkeld;

Monzievaird, near Crieff; St Martins, near Scone; and at Tullypowrie, near Atholl – the last also being cup-marked. In his excellent booklet, *A Simple Introduction to Stone Circles and Standing Stones of Perthshire*, David Watson claims there are *"no fewer than five 'witch's stones' in the county"*, but I have been unable to track down quite where the fifth one is located.

A good example of a stone circle, which is also easy to see, is at Killin, a village situated at the western head of Loch Tay, which is now in Stirlingshire but was previously in Perthshire. It is in the grounds of Kinnell House.

Then there are souterrains and cists. A souterrain is an Iron Age underground stone-lined tunnel which may have been used as a larder or even somewhere to hide in times of danger. There are three in Kinross-shire at Classochie, Hatchbank and Nether Tillyrie, but unfortunately, they are only visible as crop marks in aerial photographs.

A cist had a different function altogether. It is a much smaller, stone-lined hole in the ground which was used as a coffin or ossuary. They also contained pottery vessels holding food to sustain the dead on their journey to the next world. The custom at that time was to let the body decompose until only bones were left. The remains would be placed in the cist, which was then covered with a cairn, slab of stone or standing stone of some sort. There is a large standing stone at Fowlis Wester near Crieff called 'Ossian's Stone'. It is 7.5 feet long and 5 feet wide and originally covered a 2-feet square cist which had been full of burnt bones. However, 'Ossian's Stone' got in the way of the military road that General Wade was building at the time, so he had it moved.

Ossian was allegedly either an ancient Highland chieftain or a third-century poet, whose poems were found and translated in the latter half of the eighteenth century by a chap called James Macpherson. However, there is a school of thought that Macpherson made up both the poems and the very existence of anyone called Ossian. It is difficult to prove many aspects of early Scottish history one way or another as so much documentation was destroyed, first by Edward I and later by John Knox.

Iron Age brochs are the tallest prehistoric buildings in Britain and were only found in Scotland. They were originally tall tower-like structures with no windows and just one entrance, being built using a method much the same as dry stone walling. It is thought that they had a similar function to fortified homes as they had an inner circular courtyard. However, it would have been easy to storm the broch by climbing the walls, despite their height, so perhaps brochs were simply status symbols. We shall never know now.

Nothing remains of the cist now, but its huge cover can still be seen in the field where it was put by General Wade's troops.

Most of them are to be found on the Northern and Western Isles – in fact one in the Shetlands has survived almost intact and is 44 feet high! However, there are the remains of just one in Perth & Kinross, which is classified as a 'Scheduled Monument':

Little Dunsinane, broch ¾ mile east of Balmalcolm, Strathmore.

Latitude: 56.4785/56°28'42" N
Longitude: -3.2638/3°15'49" W

OS Eastings: 322252
OS Northings: 732533
OS Grid: NO222325

And finally, it is pertinent to mention rock art in this section, or 'cup and ring' as it is also known. This type of artwork can be over 3,000 years old, and examples are to be found all over the world, from Australia to Korea, Africa and Europe, as well as Scotland and other parts of the UK. There are believed to be between 2,000 and 3,000 'cup and ring' carvings in the country and more are being found all the time. Historic Environment Scotland has been awarded a grant by the Arts & Humanities Research Council towards a five-year project (started in 2018) to put together a database that lists them all.

In Perth & Kinross, this Neolithic and early Bronze Age rock art can be found wherever there are rocks. They are not always easy to see, often being covered in moss. A few experts have said that the rocks show up a bit more clearly when the sun is low in winter, and when the rocks are wet. Quite why the artwork was made remains uncertain, although there are many theories. Its complexity varies widely too. It can be as simple as one or two holes (cups) ground into a rock, to a much larger number of them forming an elaborate pattern, with some or all of them surrounded by one or more circles (rings).

CHAPTER TWENTY-FOUR

'A fig for those by law protected'

SUFFRAGETTES

Q UEEN VICTORIA would definitely not have been amused by the suffragettes, as she held very traditional views about a woman's place in the home, in society and she was against the idea of women voting. The suffragettes did not care what she might have thought, they were not above taking their message direct to the highest in the land.

DARING OUTRAGE AT PERTH~
WOMAN ON THE KING'S MOTOR ~ SOLDIER
TO THE RESCUE

THE ROYAL PROGRESS through Perth yesterday was marked by several suffragist incidents. One of them was of an alarming nature, and quite unprecedented, a woman getting into close proximity to their Majesties. She sprang on to the footboard of the royal motor and attempted to break the glass of the windows, inside which sat the King and Queen. She was dragged off by the police, however, before she succeeded, and amid a wild outburst of indignation by the spectators, who, but for the protection of the police and a squadron of the Scottish Horse, would have roughly handled her. She was marched off to the Police Office. This extraordinary and daring attempt to intimidate royalty – perhaps the most daring that has occurred in the history of the women's suffrage agitation – was made by a young woman, who gave her name at the bar of the Police Office as Rhoda Fleming (27 years of age), and her address as 502 Sauchiehall Street, Glasgow.

NOR DID IT STOP THEM putting up signs for her grandson, George V, to see during his visit to Perth in July 1914 when he and Queen Mary came to formally open Perth Royal Infirmary. They said, *"Welcome to your majesty's torture chamber in Perth prison"*. The reason Perth Prison was referred to as a 'torture chamber' was because with just one exception, any suffragette who went on hunger strike in a Scottish jail was sent to Perth prison to be force fed. If a woman was deemed too ill or too weak to be able to tolerate being force fed (which could be done orally, or via the anus if the oral route proved impossible or dangerous), she would be released for long enough to regain her strength and then jailed again. The action was carried out by Dr Hugh Ferguson Watson, a prison service doctor, with the voluntary help of a female warder and the matron of a Dundee nursing home. Despite his actions relating to force feeding suffragettes, Dr Watson does come across as a compassionate man who found this part of his job distasteful.

On the whole, the people of Perth did not think very highly of the suffragette movement. They showed their displeasure when two women arrived from the Dundee branch to hold an open-air meeting. The women were met by a crowd that was so hostile they needed police protection. When two suffragettes tried to speak a little later in the day, they were pelted with mud and assorted rubbish. Then the crowd turned really nasty and the police had to bring their batons into action to protect themselves and the two women.

A month later, two more suffragettes arrived from Dundee and experienced a similar reception, but not as belligerent as the first. It was bad enough, however, to warrant police help again. Maybe the good people of Perth found it difficult to forgive the suffragettes for burning down the grandstand at their racecourse or defacing their golf course greens by using acid to burn 'Votes for Women' into the grass.

On 15th February 2018, the Royal Mail released a set of commemorative postage stamps to mark 100 years since the 1918 Representation of the People Act which enfranchised some 8.4 million women aged 30 and over. (It was another ten years before women were fully enfranchised.) One of the stamps (value £1.57) features Sophia Duleep Singh selling the *Votes for Women* newspaper at Hampton Court. She was the youngest daughter of 'The Black Prince of Perthshire', who is mentioned in the section on royal associations with Perth & Kinross.

CHAPTER TWENTY-FIVE

'Fulfils great Nature's plan'

Trees and Hedges

The Royal Forestry Society describes 'Champion Trees' as, "individual trees which are exceptional examples of their species because of their enormous size, great age, rarity or historical significance".

PERTH & KINROSS IS KNOWN AS 'Big Tree Country', which is hardly surprising when you consider that its 200,000-plus acres of woodlands, contain more 'Champion Trees' than anywhere else in the UK.

At 206.69 feet, the tallest tree in Perth & Kinross is an *abies grandis* or grand fir which is at Blair Castle, Pitlochry. The widest redwood in Britain is to be found at Cluny House Gardens, north of Aberfeldy. Its girth is 36 feet, and the tree is over 130 years old.

The oldest tree in Scotland, and probably in the whole of Europe, is a yew in the churchyard at Fortingall, near Aberfeldy. It is estimated to be between 2,000 and 5,000 years old. The large disparity in its probable age is due to a measurement of the yew's various trunks in 1769. Back then, it had a total circumference of 52 feet which led to the conclusion at the time that the tree was up to 5,000 years old. Today, the yew's estimated age is considered to be between 2,000 and 3,000 years. Still pretty ancient nonetheless, but the years have taken their toll and all you can see today are the remnants of the original tree and some side shoots.

The Fortingall Yew is a male tree and despite its advanced years, it would seem that there is life in the old boy yet! He has decided to undergo a sex change. Female yews have bright red berries from autumn into winter, but the Fortingall Yew has never had them ... until now. When a little group of three berries was spotted in the upper branches of this ancient tree, it came as something of a surprise to scientists from Edinburgh's Royal Botanic Garden, despite the fact that sex changes in conifers aren't too unusual.

Another elderly tree is the Birnam Oak, found growing on the outskirts of the Perthshire village of Birnam, near Dunkeld. These days it is supported by what might best be described as 'arboreal crutches'. The wood in which this oak tree stands was mentioned by the three witches in *Macbeth*, Shakespeare's 'Scottish play', when they predicted that Macbeth would not be defeated until *"Birnam wood remove to Dunsinane"*. Although tradition has it that this oak is the last survivor of that wood, this is very unlikely. Oaks can, indeed, live to a great age, some of them for centuries, but they are nothing like as long-lived as yews. The tree you see in Birnam Wood would not have been around when Shakespeare wrote his famous play and was certainly not there 1,000 years ago when Macbeth claimed his throne.

While you are in the Dunkeld area, it is worth a trip to Dunkeld Cathedral to see a Douglas fir growing beside it. This tree has the biggest girth of its species in the UK at 23 feet.

Not so old, but certainly much more poignant, is David McCabe's spruce. During the First World War, Lieutenant David McCabe pulled saplings from the mud of no-man's-land at Passchendaele – and sent them home to his father in Perthshire. David died from wounds in 1917 and never returned to see one of these young trees grow on to splendid maturity. The saplings travelled in an ammunition box together with a letter which read:

> *"Owing to the amount of shell, rifle and machine gun fire which the place has been subject to, practically nothing is alive which is any taller than the trees I sent ... some of the fiercest fighting of the war having taken place in their vicinity".*

Today, David's tree stands as a magnificent living memorial at Abercairny Estate, Crieff. In summer 2017, a wreath was fashioned from its cones. A team of cadets cycled from Crieff to France to lay it on the grave of Lieutenant McCabe.

While you are still in the Dunkeld area, head to Craigvinean, Scotland's oldest managed forest, which has been grown from seeds planted by the nature-loving 'planting dukes' of Atholl. Craigvinean Forest forms part of the Tay Forest Park and is situated a mile north of Dunkeld. Between them, the 'tree-loving' dukes were responsible for planting about 27 million conifers in Dunkeld and round about the town, over a period of 100 years across the eighteenth and nineteenth centuries. The forest itself is home to beech trees and larches, as well as Scots pines. The forests were not planted for altruistic reasons though, but as somewhere for deer to roam; the deer were viewed more as livestock and would end up on the dinner table. At that time, the animals were not the sporting trophies they were to become from the late nineteenth century onwards.

If some of the trees seem to be growing in quite inaccessible places, not all the original seeds found their way there with the help from passing birds. The 3rd Duke of Atholl gave some assistance by loading seed into a cannon and shooting them into areas he could not reach himself, particularly in the Hermitage woodland, mentioned next.

You get a real feel for why Perth & Kinross is called 'Big Tree Country' if you visit the Hermitage, near Dunkeld. There, at one time, you could have seen a special Douglas fir, the first tree in Britain ever to grow to 200 feet – dwarfing Nelson's Column. It remained one of the tallest trees in Britain for some time. Unfortunately, 'Friday the Thirteenth' was a bad day for it. In 2017, the poor tree was blown over in a gale, smashing the notice board containing its personal details on its way down. It is sad when you consider that this tree was planted in the 1750s and that Douglas firs can live for up to 500 years. In the grounds of Scone Palace, there is a Douglas fir which was raised from a seed sent to them in 1826 by their former employee, David Douglas, after whom this fir tree was named.

The tallest Sitka spruce in Britain grows in Strathearn. It is 200 feet tall. And the tallest Japanese larch in Britain is in Diana's Grove at Blair Castle, near Blair Atholl. There are more than 20 trees there topping 150 feet.

At 5.00pm on the 28th of January 1716, a Jacobite army led by Lord George Murray, marched into Dunning and set fire to

the whole village, as they did to several other villages between Perth and Stirling. Just a few short months later, a wild hawthorn tree was planted in the village to commemorate the event. It was to remain there for the next 220 years before finally succumbing to the forces of nature and old age. The villagers wanted to replace their symbolic tree and over the succeeding years four new thorn trees were planted, but none sur-vived for long. Then a tree that had originally grown in the same place that the very first tree came from was planted. It is still happily growing in Thorntree Square where its pre-decessors once stood.

The *Guinness Book of Records* recognises the Meikleour Beech Hedge as the highest and longest hedge in the world at 100 feet at its tallest and 1,738 feet long. If you are travelling on the A93 (Blairgowrie-Perth road) you will drive right past it. As with David McCabe's spruce, there is a certain poignancy to this hedge too. It is thought to have been planted by men who later took part in the Battle of Culloden (1746), where the Jacobite forces were routed. Not one of those men returned to the Meikleour Estate, so in a way it acts as a memorial to them.

CHAPTER TWENTY-SIX

'I think on him that's far awa'

TWIN TOWNS

The very earliest occurrence of town twinning was many centuries ago in AD836, between Paderborn, Germany and Le Mans, France. Modern town twinning started in the 1920s, with 'sister' relationships beginning even earlier in the twentieth century. After the Second World War, these ideas grew to encourage both cultural and commercial links with other countries.

Here are towns in Perth & Kinross and their twinned partners.

ABERNETHY is twinned with **Grisy-Suisnes**, which is 28 miles south-east of Paris in the department of Seine-et-Marne, Île-de-France region. It is a small town located in north central France whose inhabitants are known as 'Grisysoliens'. The population of Grisy-Suisnes is a little over 2,000.

BLAIRGOWRIE is twinned with the Canadian town of **Fergus**, Ontario, which is 67 miles west of Toronto – 50 miles as the crow flies. The town lies on the Grand River and every year there is a Scottish Festival & Highland Games that celebrates local Scottish heritage. Fergus has a population of over 20,000 Blairgowrie's second twin is in the US: **Pleasanton**, California, located 39 miles south-east of San Francisco. Pleasanton describes itself as, *"a major suburb"* with over *"1,200 acres of surrounding parks, open space and trails* [which] *offer spectacular vistas and abundant recreational opportunities"*. Pleasanton itself *"is a charming historic destination"*. The population of Pleasanton is over 70,000.

COMRIE like Blairgowrie has chosen Canada for its twin. **Carleton Place**, Ontario, is about 29 miles west of Ottawa. It was first settled in the early nineteenth century when it was known as Morphy's Falls after the family who built a mill there – utilising the power of a nearby waterfall. It was renamed Carleton Place (after a street in Glasgow) when a post office was constructed. With the arrival of the railway, the town grew. Carleton Place's claim to fame is that Captain Arthur Roy Brown, DSC and Bar (the man who is officially credited by the Royal Air Force with shooting down the Red Baron in World War I) was born there. The population of Carleton Place is over 10,600.

DULL is appropriately paired with **Boring**. It is 12 miles south-east of Portland, Oregon, USA, and was named after William Harrison Boring, a Union soldier and pioneer whose family first settled the area in 1856 in the Oregon Territory. In 2013, Boring also teamed up with **Bland Shire** in New South Wales, Australia, to encourage travel to the three towns deemed the 'League of Extra-ordinary Communities'. Dull has a population of about 80.

ERROL is twinned with **Mardié**, France, which is about 91 miles south of Paris in the Centre-Loire Valley region. Mardié has a population of over 2,500.

KINROSS is twinned with the small town of **Gacé**, which lies some 93 miles west of Paris, in the Normandy region. Gacé has a population of over 2,000.

PERTH has undergone twinning with no fewer than six towns, each in a different country including Perth, Canada and Perth, Australia. Perth is also associated with:

- **Aschaffenburg**, a German town situated some 25 miles south-east of Frankfurt. Aschaffenburg straddles the River Main and its name originally meant 'castle at the ash tree river'. As with Perth & Kinross, Roman legions were stationed here (around AD700). There were two settlements in the region – Uburzis (now Würzburg) and Ascapha (now Aschaffenburg).

  Aschaffenburg hosts numerous festivals, fairs, exhibitions, markets and concerts throughout the year. The population of the town is around 69,000.

- **Bydgoszcz**, Poland, sits 188 miles north-west of Warsaw. It lies on the Brda and Vistula rivers. It is an architecturally rich city, with a wide variety of styles represented. Bydgoszcz has a population of 470,000.

- **Pskov**, Russia, is 454 miles north-west of Moscow. It lies at the confluence of the Velikaya and the Pskova rivers and is one of the most ancient Russian cities, known for its medieval architecture. Much of its thirteenth-century city wall still survives, as do many of its old churches. The population of Pskov is about 207,500.

- **Haikou**, China, lies on Hainan island 290 air miles southwest of Hong Kong and is the island's capital. Its old town quarter features a mix of Chinese and colonial European architecture. Haikou's population is just over two million.

PITLOCHRY is twinned with **Confolens**, France. On the River Vienne, at its confluence with the Goire River, amid rolling country hills, Confolens is 259 miles southwest of Paris. The town has a thirteenth-century granite bridge with ten arches (although significantly modified and repaired in the eighteenth century) and there is an ancient spring at the end of the bridge. The population of Confolens is just over 2,800.

CHAPTER TWENTY-SEVEN

'Freedom and Whisky gang thegither!'

WHISKY

At one time Perthshire was littered with whisky distilleries, many of them illicit. Today, there are just six that produce the nectar known as single malt Scotch whisky and one that used to be in Perthshire but isn't now. They include the oldest distillery in Scotland – Glenturret in Crieff – which claims to be the only whisky distillery in Scotland to hand mash during its production process. Perthshire is also home to the smallest whisky distillery in the country – Edradour at Pitlochry.

OLDEST

THE GLENTURRET DISTILLERY was not the first to use the waters of the Pitillie Burn to make its whisky. Another had been located there before it but has long since disappeared. The Glenturret Distillery very nearly did too. Established in 1775, it initially went under the name Hosh. It was licensed in 1818 but changed its name to Glenturret in its centenary year. 1921 saw the distillery close down and its equipment dismantled during the years of the Great Depression. In the late 1950s, whisky enthusiast and businessman James Fairlie acquired the premises and revived its fortunes. A great believer in traditional crafts, Fairlie endeavoured to preserve the original methods of producing whisky. Today, Glenturret still produces its whisky using hand mashing, gentle fermentation, slow distillation and cutting by eye, rather than automating every process. When the company produced a whisky named after Fairlie in 2015 – The James Fairlie Edition – it sold out in two hours.

There are two statues worth viewing at the Glenturret Distillery. As this is the distillery which also produces Famous Grouse blended whisky, it is hardly surprising to see a large bronze statue of that bird at the entrance to the car park. And look out for a bronze statue of a cat. This is Towser, a 24-year-old tortoiseshell female cat, whose job it was to keep down the mouse population in the still house where the distillery's malted barley is kept. She did such a remarkable job that she made it into the *Guinness Book of Records* by catching over 28,000 mice. Guinness estimated her total catch by sending someone to the distillery, watching her for a few days, counting how many mice she caught in that time and doing a few calculations to estimate her total catch over the years. Towser died in 1987, having done a sterling job for the company, and a number of successors have followed her into the still house. In 2017, a limited edition 'Bottle Your Own' whisky came from the Towser Cask (£85 per bottle from the distillery shop – £5 from each purchase is donated to the Snow Leopard Trust).

SMALLEST

THE EDRADOUR DISTILLERY represents a man's dream and his determination to make that dream come true. Andrew Symington owned Signatory Vintage, an independent bottling company based in Edinburgh. However, he wanted to add a distillery to his business interests but had been unsuccessful in acquiring any of the bigger ones that had come on to the market. Symington knew the Edradour Distillery very well, having taken many guests to visit the place over a ten-year period; and so, he decided to try to buy it. He contacted its owners, the Pernod Ricard group, on a number of occasions, but was told each time that it was not for sale. Symington took to phoning them every six months to check if the situation had changed and eventually it did. His persistence had paid off and he finally acquired the Edradour Distillery in 2002 (for £5.4 million).

Edradour Distillery is named after the burn that flows through it – the word 'Edradour' coming from the Gaelic for 'King Edred's Stream'.

Edradour was originally a typical farm distillery, started in 1825 by a group of eight farmers. There were many illegal distilleries in the area, as there were all over Scotland, but just two years earlier the Excise Act had come into force. This Act legalised whisky distilling for a licence fee of £10 (just over a £1,000 in today's money) and payment per gallon of proof spirit. The farmers chose to go the legal route, paid for a licence and set up their distillery in Pitlochry, calling it Glenforres. Twelve years later saw a change of name and Edradour was born.

It was to be the next century before the first Edradour single malt whisky appeared, only blends being available until then. The varieties were expanded under Andrew Symington's guidance and have grown to include five different ranges.

One of the earlier blends, many decades before Andrew Symington's involvement, was on its way to America in 1941. It was called 'King's Ransom' and was aboard a ship called the S.S. *Politician* which left Liverpool on the 3rd of February heading for Kingston, Jamaica and New Orleans, USA. Gale force winds drove the ship further and further off course until at 7.40am on the 5th of February 1941 she foundered on sandbanks off Rosinish Point, Isle of Eriskay in the Hebrides. In Hold No.5 were 264,000 bottles of Edradour whisky, many of which were gratefully salvaged by the islanders. Later action by the local police to try to recover some of the booty resulted in a number of prosecutions. This incident was used by Compton Mackenzie for his book *Whisky Galore*, and later for the film of the same name. But that's not the end of the story. Eight bottles were retrieved from the wreck by a local diver in 1987 and two of them were sold at auction, realising £12,000.

This remarkable story took yet another twist in 2001 when papers released by the Public Records Office showed that the same Hold No. 5 had also contained £145,000 in ten-shilling notes bound for Jamaica – that's several million pounds in today's money. In June 1941, just a few short months after the wreck took place, two different banks in Liverpool reported being presented with water damaged Jamaican 10-shilling notes. By 1943, they were turning up in London, Stoke-on-Trent and northern Scotland. By 1958, 211,267 of the original 290,000 notes had been recovered, while a further 2,329 had been presented to banks worldwide. Unaccounted for, even now, is £38,202 and 24,000 bottles of Edradour whisky.

NEWEST

IT HAS BEEN A GOOD 100 OR SO YEARS since Scotch whisky has seen the level of investment that exists now. Five new distilleries were opened in Scotland in 2013 and that number has been increasing each year, with 18 distilleries opening in 2017. The Perth Distilling Company, the newest one in Perthshire at the time of writing, opened in late 2017 at Aberargie, 7 miles south of Perth. Its Aberargie single malt is classed as a Lowland whisky because the distillery is just a few miles short of the line above which it could be classified as a Highland whisky.

DEWAR'S ABERFELDY DISTILLERY

ALTHOUGH DEWAR'S DOES PRODUCE SOME single malts such as Aberfeldy Highland Single Malt Scotch Whisky, it is best known for its blended products. Only one brand of blended whisky has held a Royal Warrant of Appointment granted by every monarch who has reigned since Queen Victoria (except Edward VIII who abdicated before he had time to grant any royal warrants at all). That brand is Dewar's.

The company was founded by John Dewar at some time in the mid-nineteenth century. It is uncertain quite when he began to offer his blended whiskies for sale, but when he started his business he did not have a distillery at all. Instead he bought whiskies in, then blended and bottled them before selling them on. The distillery only came into existence after his death when two of his sons took over the business. Dewar's second eldest son, also John, looked after the production and business side of things with great competence. It was his brother Thomas (Tommy) however who was the driving force behind raising the brand's profile worldwide and sending sales surging ever upward.

Tommy was quite a character. He is thought to have been only the third person in Britain to have bought a motor car. In 1892, aged just 28, he went on a two-year-long world trip to promote the company. He returned after travelling to some 30 countries and having recruited a large international sales force. Tommy's energetic approach to sales and marketing ensured the ever-growing success of Dewar's. His dynamic and imaginative promotion of the company has been continued by his successors over the years. Today, Dewar's White Label is the fifth best-selling blended Scotch in the world and the leading blended Scotch in the USA.

At home in Scotland, adopting Tommy's progressive approach in a different arena has resulted in part of the distillery being turned into a museum which offers an innovative, high-tech, multi-media experience, enabling visitors to study some items in greater detail than might otherwise have been the case. With his proven love of a pioneering, state-of-the-art approach, I cannot help thinking that Tommy would have loved the museum and his company's progress.

Both brothers were made baronets and later raised to the peerage as barons; and both served as Members of Parliament.

THE BLAIR ATHOL DISTILLERY

FOR 22 YEARS IN THE MID-NINETEENTH CENTURY Blair Athol Distillery was run by a woman, Elizabeth Conacher. She inherited it in 1860 and it was eventually sold to Peter Mackenzie & Co. in 1882 (some sources say it was 1886). The business had first been opened in 1798 by John Stewart and Robert Robertson, but soon closed down. For a while it was up and running again when John Robertson acquired it c.1825, but it foundered again ten years later. As a business it has had very mixed fortunes, closing down, only to be bought and opened up again by a number of different owners over the years and not really flourishing until the twentieth century. Even the spelling of its name changed when a former Duke of Atholl made it clear that he did not want his name associated with alcohol, despite the fact that the distillery was located in Pitlochry 7 miles away from the duke's small town of Blair Atholl. Consequently, the distillery obliged and dropped the final 'l' from its name to distinguish it from the 'grumpy' duke. There is another, more academic theory about the origin of the name Blair Athol, which maintains that it comes from the Gaelic 'Blar Ath Fhoda'. The theory suggests that early emigrants from north Ulster to western Scotland moved inland to a place they called 'Ath Fotla', or 'Second Ireland', just as later emigrants named the places they settled in after their former homes – think of Perth, Australia for example. 'Blair Athol' is simply a corruption of 'Blar Ath Fhoda'.

As with Dewar's, most of Blair Athol's whisky production is destined to become part of the company's range of blended whisky. Fortunately, every now and again a single malt becomes available. One such single malt was included in a collection to showcase Scotland's various whiskies, known as 'Flora and Fauna' because of the theme of the various label illustrations. The Blair Athol bottle had a picture of an otter, alluding to the name of the burn that supplies the distillery's water, 'Allt Dour', which translates from the Gaelic as 'Otter Burn'. This burn flows into the River Tummel, which itself flows into the River Tay. As the Tay and its tributaries host a healthy population of otters these days, it is more than likely that the same applied in the past, as evidenced by the name of the burn and that of the original business founded by John Stewart and Robert Robertson in 1798, the Aldour Distillery.

TULLIBARDINE

ALTHOUGH THE TULLIBARDINE DISTILLERY, which takes its name from the moor behind it, was only founded in 1949 the location itself has a longstanding history of indulging people's desire for a bevvy or two. It is reputed to be the first place in Scotland to brew beer (over 500 years ago).

The first 'Publick' breweries (commercial sellers) began to appear in Scotland in the fifteenth century, and the Tullibardine brewery's reputation had reached the ears of the 15-year-old James IV. He paid a visit to the brewery either on his way to his coronation in 1488, or on his way back – opinions differ. Either way, the Tullibardine Distillery is rightly proud of its royal connection.

Luckily, a few years after the young king's visit, the exchequer roll of 1494, which was used to raise funds for the royal coffers, only mentioned whisky, not beer. I wonder if the king influenced this oversight because he had enjoyed his trip to the brewery so much. James IV grew up to become a good influence in Scotland helping, for example, to bring the printing press to his country. A well-educated man himself, he also established several colleges and built a strong navy.

It was the quality of the water which has filtered down from the area's 400-million-year-old hills that first brewers, then distillers, found so irresistible. Tullibardine draws its water from the Danny Burn which takes 15 years to make its way down to the burn from the Ochil Hills behind the distillery. Gold was mined from these hills once upon a time, but now the gold is found in the form of Tullibardine's various single malt whiskies.

The Tullibardine Distillery describes itself as producing 'artisanal whisky'. And goes on to say, "*this means no shortcuts are taken; we still continue to operate the distillery without modern day computer technology*". It has a capacity of well over two million litres per annum using these methods.

THE DEANSTON DISTILLERY

ALTHOUGH IT IS TODAY SITUATED in the Stirling Council area, the Deanston Distillery, located near the village of Doune, was in Perthshire until the boundary changes, so I feel justified in including it here.

Sir Richard Arkwright, the pioneer of the modern industrial factory system and a clever entrepreneur, designed the original mill building which started spinning cotton in 1785 and only stopped in 1964. The name 'Deanston' however goes back very much further than the distillery which occupies the building now. The land on which it stands was inherited by the Dean of Dunblane in 1500. His title was coupled with the Gaelic word for a farm or settlement – 'toun' and gradually corrupted to become 'Deanston'.

Originally a flax mill stood on the site. This was converted by John Buchanan and his siblings into a water-powered carding and roving factory for converting flax into linen (Scottish-grown flax being among the best in the world). Then along came Arkwright and the cotton mill was soon up and running, initially known as the Adelphi Mill. Its next incarnation was in 1969 when manufacturing began again, but this time the end product was whisky, which still only uses Scottish grown barley. The very first single malt produced at the distillery was named 'Bannockburn'.

As with so many distilleries, ownership of the Deanston Distillery has changed on a number of occasions, the distillery first belonging to Brodie Hepburn (who also owned the Tullibardine Distillery at one point). As with some other distilleries, it was forced to shut down for a while, closing in 1982 as sales of whisky slumped generally. It went back into full production in 1991.

The distillery's water source is the River Teith and the factory was originally powered by four large waterwheels 36 feet 6 inches in diameter and 10 feet 10 inches wide. The river they turned in flows into the River Forth – although there are those who maintain that it is the other way around and that it is the Forth which is a tributary of the Teith. Half a mile south-west of Doune a bridge that was built in 1535 crosses the river. It was constructed by Robert Spittal, a tailor to Mary, Queen of Scots. The story goes that it was built by the tailor out of spite when the ferryman refused to take him across the river. You can hardly blame the ferryman, he must have heard *"Sorry, I've forgotten my purse"* too many times.

Bringing Deanston's story right up to date, its whisky is organic, and it can also claim to be helping to reduce climate change. All of its power is generated by a turbine house and its excess electricity is sold to the National Grid. It always was at the forefront of modern development. The original factory had gas lighting in the same year as Westminster Bridge in London – months earlier in fact.

* * *

WHISKY TRIVIA

- During the whisky making process, up to 70 per cent of the flavour and colour will come from the wood of the cask.

- The saying goes that whisky (whiskey if you are Irish) was invented in Ireland, but the Scots perfected it.

- Tradition has it that whisky occasionally formed part of the rent paid for Perthshire Highland farms some centuries ago, but I have not been able to verify that.

- The earliest record of distilling in Scotland was in 1494, when an entry in the Exchequer Rolls stated, *"Eight bolls of malt to Friar John Cor (in Fife) wherewith to make aqua vitae* [Latin for 'water of life']". This was enough malt to produce 1,500 bottles of whisky, and clearly indicates that distilling had already become a well-established practice in Scotland.

- The Scottish Parliament introduced the first taxes on malt and its end product in the seventeenth century. Ever increasing rates of taxation on whisky were applied following the Union with England Act 1707, which led to moves to tame rebellious Scottish clans. So, the clans took to producing whisky illegally in stills hidden in the heather-clad hills and mountains. Signalling systems from one hilltop to another warned of excise officers patrolling the area. Today, Scotch whisky is taxed more heavily than any other alcoholic drink – the government taking more than 75 per cent of a bottle's selling price in tax.

- By the 1820s, despite the fact that as many as 14,000 illicit stills were being confiscated every year, more than half the whisky consumed in Scotland was being enjoyed without payment of duty.

- Today, Scotch whisky is so popular that exports earn over £125 every second, with 38 bottles making their way abroad in the same timescale.

- Over 40,000 jobs right across the UK exist thanks to the Scotch whisky industry.

- Scotch whisky is sold in around 200 markets worldwide.

- In Spain, whisky often has cola added to it, rather than water which is favoured in Britain.

- More Scotch is sold in one month in France, than cognac in a year.

- Various types of whisky are produced in countries as far apart as North America (both Canada and the USA), Japan, Sweden, Belgium, Liechtenstein, the Antipodes, South Africa and Taiwan.

CHAPTER TWENTY-EIGHT

'Give me ae spark o' Nature's fire'

Wildlife

Wolves, lynx, beavers and bears all once roamed around Perth & Kinross's ancient forests.

There is some debate about whether wolves were finally killed off in the seventeenth or the eighteenth century. But I love the story Jeremy Duncan recounts in his book *Perth and Kinross: The Big County* about the demise of the last wolf in the region. Duncan tells of an alleged incident near Crieff in 1710 when a wolf attempted to run off with a woman's baby. The nearest weapon to hand was a wooden potato masher and the woman bashed the wolf on the right ear with it, killing the animal. Duncan ponders whether it was the force of the blow that killed it or *"sheer surprise at the choice of weapon"*.

I doubt if that counted as 'hunting them down' as stipulated by the Act passed by James I intended to rid Scotland entirely of wolves once and for all. Under his Act, wolf hunts were to be carried out between St Mark's Day (25th of April) and Lammas (1st of August) – in other words when wolves are with pups, which would therefore also die, since their dead parents would not be around to feed them.

It is debatable whether it was hunting or the loss of much of their extensive Caledonian forest habitat that was to blame for the wolf's extinction. There have been calls by various organisations and individuals to reintroduce both the wolf and lynx to Scotland. However, this requires approval by Scottish Natural Heritage, the government organisation responsible for wildlife and habitats in Scotland, and at the time of writing there are no such plans.

There have been some successful reintroductions of birds and animals which had previously become extinct in the region. Beaver, for example, which became extinct in the Highlands after the fifteenth century, were brought back to the area by Scottish National Heritage ten years ago and are now thriving in Perth & Kinross, with an estimated 38 or 39 beaver territories in the Tay catchment area, particularly on the River Earn. If you are visiting Loch of the Lowes between May and August, you might be lucky enough to see a beaver or two.

The Tay and its tributaries also support a healthy population of otters, as there are plenty of eels, lamprey, salmon, trout and frogs for them to eat. You would not normally expect to see these creatures anywhere but near their natural watery habitat, but in December 2015 one was seen on Mill Street in the middle of Perth. Maybe it was looking in shop windows trying to get some ideas for Christmas presents, or checking out the programme at the concert hall.

Three quarters of the UK's red squirrels are to be found in Scotland. Sadly, even here they are under threat from grey squirrels which were introduced to the UK from North America in the late nineteenth century. Red squirrels can be seen in a number of places in Perth & Kinross, but the observation hide at Loch of the Lowes offers an excellent chance to watch them visit the squirrel feeder; March to November is the best time to see them there.

The Scottish wildcat is Britain's most endangered species and protected under law. The chance of you seeing one is so remote that you might be better viewing one of the many wildcat videos uploaded to *YouTube* and watching this beautiful creature on screen. Or, if you do not mind seeing them in captivity, a visit to Auchingarrich Wildlife Centre, near Comrie is worthwhile. It is slightly easier to see pine martens, but in case you are not lucky, *YouTube* delivers again.

Other mammals to be seen in Perth & Kinross include red deer (Britain's largest indigenous animal), roe and fallow deer, and the badger.

As well as salmon, trout and various types of lamprey, there is another interesting creature to be found in the River Tay Special Area of Conservation and that is the freshwater pearl mussel – a critically endangered mollusc and therefore protected. Freshwater pearl mussels can live for up to 100 years if not disturbed and, again if undisturbed, can grow as large as a human hand. Due to a century of illegal pearl fishing, a decline in water quality and the disruption of their habitat, these creatures are losing the battle to survive.

The last white-tailed sea eagle was shot in 1918 in Shetland. They were reintroduced in 1975 to the Inner Hebrides and successfully expanded their range. Between 2007 and 2012, the white-tailed sea eagle was also introduced to Scotland's East Coast and spread out from there. During the bad weather of winter 2017-18 (termed 'The Beast from the East'), five of these white-tailed sea eagles took off for a bit of a respite at the west coast and remarkably remembered to return home after their holiday. In Spring of 2018, a sea eagle went missing in the Dunkeld area after its satellite tag stopped working. The RSPB joined forces with Police Scotland and a number of local gamekeepers to try to establish what had happened to it. At the time of writing, there has been no further news.

Another bird of prey became extinct long before the white-tailed sea eagle. The last red kite was exterminated in Scotland in 1870 and reintroduced in the 1980s. They are doing well, but sadly several of them are deliberately poisoned each year.

Ospreys can be seen in several locations in Perth & Kinross during the summer months, such as Loch Leven in Kinross, Loch of the Lowes, near Dunkeld, and Alyth, near Blairgowrie. Although these birds disappeared from Scotland at the beginning of the twentieth century, they were also successfully reintroduced in the 1950s. Ospreys usually arrive around April and start migrating back to Africa in August.

Next in size to the white-tailed sea eagle, the golden eagle has a wing span of 7 feet or more. It is not often seen in Eastern Scotland; you need to be up in the Highlands to stand a chance of seeing it at all.

CHAPTER TWENTY-NINE

'And there's a hand, my trusty fiere!
And gie's a hand o' thine!'

WORLDWIDE

MASS EMIGRATION from Scotland to pastures new began as
early as the end of the Jacobite risings, towards the end of the
seventeenth and early eighteenth centuries, and continued
through to the early twentieth century, when it slowed down.

T HE HIGHLAND CLEARANCES, poverty, the potato famine and
religious beliefs accounted for some of the early reasons why
people decided to leave. A more surprising reason among Lowland
emigrants was a good education. As has been mentioned in the
section about Innerpeffray Library, a remarkably high percentage of
the population of Scotland was literate, even in the seventeenth
century. This was reflected in the fact that by then the country had
five universities – not bad for a population of fewer than a million
people at the time. The universities were at St Andrews (*est.*1413),
Glasgow (*est.*1451), two in Aberdeen (*est.*1495 and *est.*1593) and
Edinburgh (*est.*1583).

There were few opportunities for all these well-educated people,
which included doctors, merchants and farmers among their number,
so they took off to try to find or create them elsewhere. It was natural
to name the places they settled after the places they came from. The
number who left the Perth & Kinross area and settled in various parts
of the world can be seen in the names they gave to their settlements,
even if some have subsequently changed.

There are 17 places called Perth in the world, including the city in
Scotland, after which they were all named.

AUSTRALIA

PERTH, WESTERN AUSTRALIA dates as a colonial settlement from December 1696 when Willem Hesselsz de Vlamingh, a Dutch sea-captain, landed close to the present-day resort of Cottesloe Beach. It was 1829 before Captain James Stirling formally founded Perth and settlers began to arrive.

PERTH, TASMANIA is located 112 miles north of the island's capital city of Hobart. The town was settled in 1821 and many of its present historic buildings date back to that time. The name Perth was chosen by a Scotsman, the then Governor of New South Wales, Major General Lachlan Macquarie. He did not bother to settle in Perth though, he was merely passing through.

CANADA

PERTH, ONTARIO witnessed the arrival of Scottish families and discharged soldiers after the Battle of Waterloo in 1815, with a good deal of 'encouragement' from the British Government of the time.

PERTH, NEW BRUNSWICK has a population of 1,096 according to the 2011 Census. It appears to be a lively village located on both banks of the Saint John River. Perth has a lot going on, including an event called the 'Gathering of the Scots'.

USA

PERTH, DELAWARE lies in the state's New Castle County.

PERTH, INDIANA grew up around the railway which reached the area in 1870. Ten years later, it got its own post office, which had an even shorter life than the one in Kansas (see below), lasting a mere 49 years.

PERTH, KANSAS had a post office in 1882, but it only lasted for 72 years, closing in 1954. The town was a shipping point for livestock on the Rock Island Railroad.

PERTH, MINNESOTA started out being called 'Iceland', but changed its name to Perth in 1905.

PERTH, MISSISSIPPI has a population of 7,726 and is a community in Jefferson County.

PERTH, NEVADA lies in the state's Pershing County.

PERTH, NEW YORK has a population of 3,646 according to the 2010 Census. Scottish pioneers settled here in about 1772.

PERTH, NORTH DAKOTA was founded in 1897 and the 2010 Census showed it then had a population of just nine people.

PERTH, VIRGINIA lies in the state's Halifax County.

REST OF THE WORLD

PERTH, JAMAICA lies just a mile or two from the regional capital of Mandeville.

PERTH, GUYANA is a village situated in the East Coast Demerara countryside of this South American country.

PERTH, SOUTH AFRICA lies in central northern South Africa, close to the Botswana border.

* * *

Other parts of Perth & Kinross also provide memories of their settlers' origins.

AUSTRALIA

ABERFELDY, VICTORIA is a small town in Victoria, which was initially known as Mount Lookout. It is 78 miles east of Melbourne and was founded in 1871 following the discovery of gold. A post office was opened the following year, but it closed in 1967. At its height, Aberfeldy had a population of about 500. Once the gold rush was over, the town was used for sheep and cattle grazing and for the production of potatoes and other crops.

BLAIRGOWRIE, VICTORIA is a seaside village 54 miles south of Melbourne. It did not have a post office until the 1st of November 1947. Blairgowrie's claim to fame is that Rhys Isaac died there in 2010. He was the first and only Australian historian to win a Pulitzer Prize; awarded for his book *The Transformation of Virginia, 1740-1790.*

DUNKELD, VICTORIA lies at the southern end of the Grampians National Park and is 176 miles west of Melbourne, in fine wool producing country. In the 2016 Census, Dunkeld had a population of 678. The *Robertson's Woolpack Inn* was the first building to be erected in 1845, then five other hotels were built soon after, to accommodate passengers from the railway. Woefully, in January 1944, fires destroyed one-third of Dunkeld's houses and only the Royal Mail Hotel remained unscathed of the original hotels. The modern town seems to be thriving, to the extent that it has an up-market restaurant and accommodation, a general store, two cafes, a post office, an art gallery, a petrol station, schools, a local museum, a bookstore, a (sandstone) stonemason, a DIY store and at least one local vineyard.

DUNKELD, QUEENSLAND lies in the Maranoa Region of Queensland and the Maranoa River flows from north to south through the area. It was named by Edward Flood and Samuel Deane Gordon in 1863.

KINROSS, WESTERN AUSTRALIA is a small suburb 20 miles north of Perth, constructed in 1992-3. According to the 2006 Census, Kinross has a population of 7,232.

SCONE, NEW SOUTH WALES is noted for breeding thoroughbred racehorses and is known as the 'Horse Capital of Australia'. In the 2006 Census, Scone had a population of 4,624.

CANADA

ONTARIO AND OTHER eastern seaboard areas seemed to have received several lots of emigrants from Perth & Kinross, if place names are anything to go by.

ABERFELDY, ONTARIO is a dispersed rural community 163 miles south-west of Toronto.

CRIEFF, ONTARIO was settled by Highland Scots in the 1830s. They cleared the land, building log cabins and barns.

KINROSS, PRINCE EDWARD ISLAND is a small community in an area with several roads named after other Scottish towns. The area fittingly produces 25 per cent of Canada's potatoes.

RANNOCH, ONTARIO sits 310 miles south-west of Ottawa.

SCONEVILLE, ONTARIO (now called Chesley) is located 400 miles south-west of Ottawa. It was originally developed around mills built on the Saugeen River in about 1858. Mostly destroyed by fire in 1888, Scone was rebuilt with brick and stone buildings instead of the wood which was the original building material.

USA

KINROSS, IOWA was created by people moving to be close to a new railroad depot in 1879. Sadly, it had a population of only 73 at the 2010 Census. Kinross is described as currently being *"essentially a ghost town, having no public businesses or schools; the large closed brick school and an abandoned gas station are the only indicators of a town"*.

KINROSS, KENTUCKY was originally a flag stop (a request stop) on the Louisville and Nashville Railroad. It is in Clark County about a mile north of Winchester.

KINROSS, MICHIGAN had a population of 7,561 at the 2010 Census. It is a charter township, which means it is allowed certain rights and responsibilities of home rule that are intermediate between those of a city and a village.

CHAPTER QUOTATIONS

All chapter quotations are by Robert Burns except for that in Chapter 7 which appropriately is from Walter Scott's novel, *The Fair Maid of Perth*.

Selected Timeline
 'Life is all a variorum' from *The Jolly Beggars*.

Thirty Bits and Pieces
 'O thou! whatever title suit thee' from *Address to the Deil*.

Battles, Skirmishes and Riots
 'See the front o' battle lour' from *March to Bannockburn*.

Castles, Palaces and Hillforts
 'But och! It hardens a' within, and petrifies the feeling!' from *Epistle to a Young Friend*.

Churches and Cathedrals
 'They never sought in vain that sought the Lord aright' from *The Cotter's Saturday Night*.

Crannogs
 'The boat rocks at the pier' from *My Bonnie Mary*.

Curling and Golf
 'Do but try to develop his hooks and his crooks' from *Sketch*, inscribed to Charles, James Fox.

Dragons, Fairies, Ghosts and Witches
 'An justifies that ill opinion which makes thee startle' from *To a Mouse*.

Fair Maid of Perth
 ''Tis but a pang, and then a thrill' from *The Fair Maid of Perth* by Sir Walter Scott.

Famous People
 'Contented wi' little and cantie wi' mair' from *Contented wi' Little*.

Festivals
 'But pleasures are like poppies spread' from *Tam o' Shanter*.

Films and Film Locations
 'But how the subject-theme may gang' from *Epistle to A Young Friend*.

Gallantry and the Victoria Cross
 'The birth-place of valour, the country of worth' from *My Heart's in the Highlands*.

Historic Pubs, Inns and Hotels
 'When drinkers drink' from *Holy Willie's Prayer*.

Hospitals
'And a' the comfort we're to get' from *The Tree of Liberty*.

Innerpeffray Library
'Come, Firm Resolve, take thou the van' from *To Dr Blacklock*.

Lord-Lieutenants
'Princes and Lords are but the breath of kings'
from *The Cotter's Saturday Night*.

Munros, Corbetts, Grahams, Donalds and Marilyns
'My heart's in the Highlands, wherever I go'
from *My Heart's in the Highlands*.

Nature Reserves
'Auld nature swears, the lovely dears her noblest work she classes'
from *Green Grow the Rashes*.

Plague
'O may 't ne'er be a living plague' from *Holy Willie's Prayer*.

Poetry
'Perhaps it may turn out a sang' from *Epistle to A Young Friend*.

Railways
'I wander in the ways of men'
from *Lament for James, Earl of Glencairn*.

Rivers, Lochs and Waterfalls
'Flow gently, I'll sing thee a song in thy praise' from *Afton Water*.

Royals
'For thus the Royal mandate ran' from *Epistle to J.L.*

Standing Stones
'His ancient, trusty, drouthy crony' from *Tam o' Shanter*.

Suffragettes
'A fig for those by law protected!' from *The Jolly Beggars*.

Tree and Hedges
'Fulfils great Nature's plan' [*sic*] from *Epistle to J.L.*

Twin Towns
'I think on him that's far awa'' from *The Farewell*.

Whisky
'Freedom and Whisky gang thegither!' [*sic*]
from *The Author's Earnest Cry and Prayer*.

Wildlife
'Give me ae spark o' Nature's fire' [*sic*] from *Epistle to J.L.*

Worldwide
'And there's a hand, my trusty fiere! And gie's a hand o' thine!'
from *Auld Lang Syne*.

SELECT BIBLIOGRAPHY

Articles, Books, Pamphlets and Papers

Abertay Historical Society (eds), *Ten Taysiders: Forgotten Figures from Dundee, Angus & Perthshire* (Dundee: Abertay Historical Society, 2011)

Aitchison. N. B., *Macbeth: Man and Myth* (Stroud: The History Press Ltd, 2000)

Ardill, Thomas, 'Burleigh Castle, Milnathort 1834 by Joseph Mallord William Turner', catalogue entry, October 2010, in David Blayney Brown (ed.), *J. M. W. Turner: Sketchbooks, Drawings and Watercolours* (London: Tate Research Publication, 2012)
[**ONLINE**] Available at https://www.tate.org.uk/art/research-publications/jmw-turner/joseph-mallord-william-turner-burleigh-castle-milnathort-r1136381

Begg, R. Burns, 'Notice of a crannog discovered in Lochleven, Kinross-shire, on 7th September 1887', *Society of Antiquaries of Scotland*, Volume 22 (1887-8)

Bowler, David P., with **R. Coleman, D. Munro, D. Perry** and **N. Robertson**, *Perth: The Archaeology and Development of a Scottish Burgh*, Monograph 3 (Perth: Tayside and Fife Archaeological Committee Perth, 2004)

Bowler, David, *The Origins of Perth: A Medieval Royal Burgh* (Perth: Perth & Kinross Heritage Trust, 2006)

Bowler, David, 'Rising from the Waves: The Development of the Historic Burgh of Perth', http://www.tafac.org.uk/floods.pdf

Colburn, Henry, *Letters of Mary, Queen of Scots (First published from the originals) Volume II by Agnes Strickland* (London, 2009)

Corbett, L., E. K. Roy and **R. C. Haddon**, *The Ochil Hills* (Stirling: Forth Naturalist & Historian, 1994)

Croose, E., J. D. S. Birks, and **H. W. Schofield**, 'Expansion zone survey of pine marten (*Martes martes*) distribution in Scotland, 2012-2013', *Scottish Natural Heritage Commissioned Report No. 520* (2013)

Day, J. P., *Clackmannan and Kinross* (Cambridge: Cambridge County Geographies, 1915)

Driscoll, Stephen T., *Alba: The Gaelic Kingdom of Scotland AD 800-1124* (Edinburgh: Birlinn with Historic Scotland, 2002)

Duncan, Jeremy, *Perth and Kinross: The Big County* (Edinburgh: John Donald Publishers Ltd, 1997)

Finley, Gerald E., 'J. M. W. Turner and Sir Walter Scott: Iconography of a tour', *Journal of the Warburg and Courtauld Institutes*, 35 (1972)

Firth, C. H., *Scotland and the Protectorate: letters and papers relating to the military government of Scotland ... from January 1654 to June 1659* (Charleston: Nabu Press, 2010)

Fittis, Robert Scott, *A Book of Perthshire Memorabilia* (Perth: Constitutional Office, 1879)

Fraser, Antonia, *Mary, Queen of Scots* (London: Weidenfeld & Nicolson, 1969)

Gordon, T. Crouther, *Robert Louis Stevenson in Pitlochry* (Scotland, 1988)

Hall, Derek, 'Unto yon hospital at tounis end' – the Scottish medieval hospital', *Tayside and Fife Archaeological Journal*, Volume 12 (2006)

Hall, James, *Travels in Scotland, by an Unusual Route – Volume I and II* (London: J. Johnson, 1807)

Hulbert, John, *Perth: A comprehensive guide for locals and visitors* (Edinburgh: Luath Press Ltd, 2015)

Leneman, Leah, *Martyrs in our midst: Dundee, Perth and the forcible feeding of suffragettes* (Dundee: Abertay Historical Society, 1993)

Liddell, Colin, *Pitlochry: heritage of a Highland district* (Perth: Perth & Kinross Libraries, 1994)

Lock, G. and **I. Raston**, *Atlas of Hillforts of Britain and Ireland* [**ONLINE**] Available at https://hillforts.arch.ox.ac.uk

McNab, John, *The Clan MacNab: a short sketch* (Edinburgh: The Clan MacNab Association, 1907)

Mitchell, Ian R., *On the trail of Queen Victoria in the Highlands* (Edinburgh: Luath Press, 2000)

Mullett, Charles F., 'Plague Policy in Scotland, 16th-17th Centuries', *Osiris*, Volume 30 (2015)

Murray, Jim, *The Complete Guide to Whisky: selecting, comparing, and drinking the world's greatest whiskies* (London: Carlton, 1997)

National Alliance Against Tolls, *Scottish Executive – Tolled Bridges Review – Consultation 2005* (2005)

O'Donnell, Elliot, *Scottish Ghost Stories* (White Press, 2016)

Oram, Richard D., 'Responses to Epidemic Disease in Sixteenth-and-Seventeenth-century Scotland', *Renaissance and Reformation*, 30, 4 (September 2006)

Perth & Kinross Heritage Trust & The Scottish Crannog Centre (author Nick Dixon), *The Crannogs of Perthshire – a Guide* (Perth: Perth & Kinross Heritage Trust, 2009)

Philippou, Paul and **Rob Hands**, *Battleground Perthshire: Two Thousand Years of Battles, Encounters & Skirmishes* (Perth: Tippermuir Books Ltd, 2009)

Philippou, Paul and **Rob Hands**, *Born in Perthshire* (Perth: Tippermuir Books Ltd, 2012)

Robertson, David and **Ian Robertson**, *Historic trees of Perthshire* (Perth: The Friends of Perth & Kinross Council Archive, 2015)

Robertson, James Alexander, *The Gaelic Topography of Scotland* (Edinburgh: W. P. Nimmo, 1874)

Robertson, James Irvine, 'Atholl, Scotland's Heartland' [ONLINE] Available at http://www.donnachaidh.com/history-atholl-scotlands-heartland.html

Scottish Natural Heritage & Scotland's National Nature Reserves, 'The Story of Abernethy – Dell Woods National Nature Reserve' [ONLINE] Available at https://www.nature.scot/sites/default/files/2018-03/The%20Story%20of%20Abernethy%20-%20Dell%20Woods%20National%20Nature%20Reserve.pdf

Scottish Natural Heritage, 'River Tay Special Area of Conservation' [ONLINE] Available at http://www.pkc.gov.uk/media/37577/River-Tay-SPG-Final-2016/pdf/River_Tay_SPG_Final_2016

Scottish National Heritage, 'Tayside Beaver Study, Group Final Report' [ONLINE] Available at https://www.nature.scot/sites/default/files/2017-11/Tayside%20Beaver%20Study%20Group%20-%20%20Final%20Report%202015.pdf

Seath, J. W. and **R. E. Seath**, *Dunbarney: a parish with a past* (Perth: Perth & Kinross District Libraries, 1991)

Short, Janice, 'Wolf's Tale – The history of the wolf in Scotland' [ONLINE] Available at http://www.wolvesandhumans.org/wolves/history_of_wolves_in_scotland.htm

Simpson, John, 'Flooding in Perth: History, Impacts and Management' (Royal Scottish Geographical Society)

[**ONLINE**] Available at https://rsgs.org/wp-content/uploads/2015/03/
Flooding-in-Perth-history-impacts-management.pdf

Smith, Gavin D. and **Dominic Roskrow**, *The Whisky Book*
(London: Dorling Kindersley, 2012)

Smith, Roger, *The Great Flood: A Chronicle of the events and people
of Perth and Kinross during the flood of January 1993*
(Perth: Perth & Kinross District Council, 1993)

Stansfield, Gordon, *Perthshire & Kinross-shire's Lost Railways*
(Catrine: Stenlake Publishing, 2001)

Tabraham, Chris, *Loch Leven Castle*, Historic Scotland Official
Souvenir Guide

The New Statistical Account of Scotland, Volume X, Perth
(Edinburgh & London: William Blackwood & Sons, 1845)

Vaughan, Geraldine, 'The Irish Famine in a Scottish Perspective
1845-1851', *Cahiers du Mimmoc*, 12 (2015)

Visit Scotland, *Perthshire: Big Tree Country* (Perth: Visit Scotland)

Walker, Nancy H. and **Andrew Thorburn**, *A Historical Guide to the
County of Kinross* (Kinross: Kinross-shire Antiquarian Society, 1980)

Walker, Nancy H., *Lochleven's Royal Prisoner: Mary, Queen of Scots*,
(Scotland: 1983)

Walker, Nancy H., *The Seven Castles in Kinross-shire* (Scotland: 1993)

Warner, Philip, *Famous Scottish Battles: where battles were fought,
why they were fought, how they were won and lost*
(New York: Barnes & Noble Books, 1996)

Watson, Angus, *The Ochils: placenames, history, tradition*
(Perth: Perth & Kinross District Libraries, 1995)

Watson, David and **Rosemary Watson**, *Simple Introduction to the
Stone Circles and Standing Stones of Perthshire*
(Scotland: Photoprint Scotland, 2007)

Withers, Charles W. J., *Gaelic Scotland: the transformation of a
culture region* (Abingdon: Taylor & Francis, 2017)

Ziegler, Philip, *The Black Death* (London: Penguin Books, 1982)

Journals, Magazines and Newspapers

Scots Magazine (October 2017)

Teesdale Mercury (24 July 1872)

Radio Programmes

In Our Time: 'The Highland Clearances' (BBC Radio 4)

Websites

https://hillforts.arch.ox.ac.uk ~ Atlas of Hillforts of Britain and Ireland

http://www.donnachaidh.com/index.html ~ Clan Donnachaidh Society

https://www.dougiemaclean.com ~ Dougie MacLean

https://www.poetryfoundation.org ~ Poetry Foundation

https://www.nature.scot ~ Scottish Natural Heritage

www.scottishpoetrylibrary.org.uk ~ Scottish Poetry Library

https://www.tate.org.uk ~ Tate (Galleries)

http://www.tafac.org.uk ~ Tayside and Fife Archaeology Committee

http://www.wolvesandhumans.org/index.htm ~ The Wolves and Humans Foundation

https://www.ed.ac.uk ~ University of Edinburgh

ABOUT THE AUTHOR

AFTER 20 YEARS of writing general interest articles on a wide variety of subjects, and editing a wildlife magazine when living abroad, Trish Colton retired 14 years ago and began to write books. Most were about local history but two were about her pet chickens. This book is her eighth and another is in the pipeline.

THE PUBLISHER

Tippermuir Books Ltd (*est.* 2009) is an independent publishing company based in Perth, Scotland.

OTHER TITLES FROM TIPPERMUIR BOOKS

Spanish Thermopylae (Paul S. Philippou, 2009)

Battleground Perthshire
(Paul S. Philippou & Robert A. Hands, 2009)

Perth: Street by Street
(Paul S. Philippou and Roben Antoniewicz, 2012)

Born in Perthshire
(Paul S. Philippou and Robert A. Hands, 2012)

In Spain with Orwell (Christopher Hall, 2013)

Trust (Ajay Close, 2014)

Perth: As Others Saw Us (Donald Paton, 2014)

Love All (Dorothy L. Sayers, 2015)

A Chocolate Soldier (David W. Millar, 2016)

The Early Photographers of Perthshire
(Roben Antoniewicz and Paul S. Philippou, 2016)

Taking Detective Novels Seriously:
The Collected Crime Reviews of Dorothy L. Sayers
(Dorothy L. Sayers and Martin Edwards, 2017)

Walking with Ghosts (Alan J. Laing, 2017)

No Fair City: Dark Tales From Perth's Past
(Gary Knight, 2017)

*The Tale o the Wee Mowdie that
wantit tae ken wha keeched on his heid*
(Werner Holzwarth and Wolf Erlbruch,
translated by Matthew Mackie, 2017)

*Hunters: Wee Stories from the Crescent:
A Reminiscence of Perth's Hunter Crescent*
(Anthony Camilleri, 2017)

Flipstones (Jim Mackintosh, 2018)

FORTHCOMING

Perth and the Jacobite Rising of 1715-16 (Kathleen Lyle, 2019)

The Piper of Tobruk (Alice Soper, 2019)

The Scots Emoji Dictionary (Michael Dempster, 2019)

William Soutar: Collected Works: Volume 1 - Poetry
(Paul S. Philippou (ed.), 2019)

BY LULLABY PRESS
(an imprint of Tippermuir Books)

A Little Book of Carol's (Carol Page, 2018)

All titles are available from bookshops and online booksellers.

They can also be purchased directly at
www.tippermuirbooks.co.uk

Tippermuir Books Ltd can be contacted at
mail@tippermuirbooks.co.uk

PERTH AND THE
"69 CITIES OF THE UK"
PROJECT

In 2016, ARTIST CARL LAVIA teamed up with photographer Lorna Le Bredonchel and together created the "69 Cities of the UK" project. The aim of the project is to produce large-size ink sketches of visited UK cities.

Towards the end of 2018, the pair reached Perth having completed sketches of Birmingham, Dundee, Edinburgh, London, Manchester, and Stirling. The completed 2 metre by 1 metre impression of Perth, which took three months to produce, went on show in early 2019.

A small section of the Perth impression is detailed on the cover of *Perth & Kinross: A Pocket Miscellany*. Prints based on the full-size sketch are available to buy from the project website: **https://www.sketchnthecity.com.**

Carl, aka Sketch, is a self-taught artist based in London. He has been sketching since the age of five, when he first became interested in the aesthetics of architecture, maps, and cityscapes. Whilst in his early work he created fictional cities, Carl's current practice focuses on depicting visited cities from an aerial viewpoint, emphasising the abstraction of pattern and intensifying the detail and abundance of information. Predominantly working with ink on archival paper, Carl distinguishes between drawing and his approach – sketching – which allows for a more immediate and impressionistic response.

Lorna studied photography at LCC, she handles creative output across all aspects including, research, mapping, photography, drone video and still photography, online presence, and securing exhibition space within each city.

During their epic road trip, Carl is sketching in large scale every single city within the UK, alongside Lorna who is documenting the entire process. Each artwork takes a month to three months create, during which time they explore the city by foot, Carl making sketches and Lorna undertaking planning, research and taking photographs. The cityscape is then created, using the small sketches and photographic fragments, using only black and white, pen on paper, to capture simultaneously the intricate details and vast expanse of the urban environment.